T0167735

Crime and punishment in nineteenth-century Belfast

Maynooth Studies in Local History

SERIES EDITOR Raymond Gillespie

This year Maynooth Studies in Local History offers its usual, if slightly attenuated, selection of explorations of the local past. These four new volumes continue the tradition of their predecessors by interrogating the local historical experience of Ireland over a wide geographical and chronological range. In doing so they not only provide insights into the specifics of the local experience that is crucial to the understanding of the evolution of Irish society but they also reveal the infinite possibilities that the study of local history presents. Chronologically this year's group of small books range from a study of the implications of the 12th-century grant of land in what is now Co. Meath by Tigernán Ua Ruairc to the revelations thrown up by the activities of the rabble rouser and parricide John Linn in early 19th-century Belfast. These were undoubtedly very different worlds: the rolling plains of Meath as opposed to the grimy industrial world of a rapidly modernizing industrial city. The contrasts between these two places could not be greater but each study engages with these realities drawing evidence from the prestigious Book of Kells on the one hand and on the murky worlds documented in prison reports and parliamentary papers on the other. Both studies contribute to understanding the socially diverse worlds of the past and help shape how we understand the way in which those who inhabited them lived their daily lives.

These contrasts are even clearer in the other two studies included in this year's offering. We encounter the world of urban Ulster as seen through the eyes of those who lived in 17th- and 18th-century Belturbet juxtaposed with the rural society that developed on the Morristown Lattin estate in Kildare. The former was dominated by Protestant settlers who had arrived as part of the Plantation of Ulster whereas the latter was an estate owned by a Catholic landowner where both landlord and tenants struggled to find a way around the restrictive legislation on Catholic leasing and ownership of property. For all their contrasts these studies share a common theme – that of groups of people struggling to come terms with new and unexpected developments. These studies stretch the historical imagination beyond a mere chronicling of events within administrative or geographical boundaries and raise questions about why these diverse places have the personality that they have developed. They represent some of the most innovative and exciting research being undertaken in Irish history today and convey the vibrancy and excitement of the world of Irish local history.

Maynooth Studies in Local History: Number 148

Crime and punishment in nineteenth-century Belfast: the story of John Linn

Jonathan Jeffrey Wright

FOUR COURTS PRESS

Set in 10pt on 12pt Bembo by
Carrigboy Typesetting Services for
FOUR COURTS PRESS LTD
7 Malpas Street, Dublin 8, Ireland
www.fourcourtspress.ie
and in North America for
FOUR COURTS PRESS
c/o IPG, 814 N Franklin St, Chicago, IL 60610

ISBN 978–1–84682–856–0

Printed in Ireland
by SprintPrint, Dublin.

Contents

Acknowledgments   6

Introduction   7

1   'A young man of ungovernable passions'   10

2   'HORRID MURDER. – PARRICIDE.'   25

3   'So mischievous and unmanageable a character'   42

Conclusion   62

Notes   67

Acknowledgments

I first encountered the story of John Linn several years ago, while working at Queen's University Belfast as a research fellow on the AHRC-funded Scientific Metropolis research project (grant number AH/J004952/1). It is a pleasure to acknowledge the support I received from Diarmid Finnegan, PI on the project, who encouraged my initial investigation of the story. More recently, Raymond Gillespie has pushed me to write the story up, and has been typically generous in bringing sources to my attention, offering advice (at times much needed) and reading draft chapters. Thanks are also due to Salvador Ryan, who provided an opportunity to revisit Linn when my file on him was beginning to gather dust, and to my friends and colleagues in the Department of History at Maynooth University, who provide such a collegial and supportive environment in which to work. I am grateful also for advice I have received from Richard Mc Mahon and Gregory O'Connor. Finally, and as always, special thanks are due to Rhiannon, for her patience and support, and to George and Clara – my favourite distractions from work.

Introduction

At 9 a.m. on the morning of 11 May 1838, the convict ship *Clyde* weighed anchor in Kingstown Harbour, Dublin. Having been 'unmoored & got ready for sea' the day previously, the ship 'stood out of the harbour [and] tacked off & on waiting for Lieut Isham the officer of the Guard'. By midday Isham had boarded the vessel and it 'made sail', beginning the long journey to New South Wales. Alongside its crew and guards, the *Clyde* carried three 'free passengers', a group of quarrelsome soldiers' wives and 215 convicts – all of them male. Included in their number were the unruly, the unfortunate and the insolent. In the journal of the ship's surgeon, John Smith, we find reference to the punishment of Ed Delanhunt, 'a bad subject', who received floggings for fighting and thieving. Likewise, we encounter an unnamed boy, described as 'a very hardened youth', who was punished for 'indecent conduct' before the *Clyde* had even left Dublin; a 'dumb man', also unnamed, who was subject to teasing from his fellow prisoners, and who was himself punished for violent outbursts on at least three occasions; and numerous others, who received punishment for sundry shipboard infractions. Save that they were hard, relatively little is known of the lives of such men. But there was one prisoner present on the *Clyde* (and mentioned in passing in Smith's journal), concerning whose life rather a good deal can be said – the subject of the present study, John Linn.[1]

A 'tall powerful man' with 'enormous muscular powers', a 'deformity in his lip' and a troubling history of violence, Linn was, at the time of his transportation to New South Wales, an infamous figure.[2] He was, as Smith put it in his journal, a 'notorious parricide'.[3] In the chapters that follow, the precise sequence of events that led Linn to the prisoners' deck of the *Clyde* will be discussed in detail, but a brief summary of his story might, at the outset, prove helpful.

Linn's journey to the *Clyde* had begun in the Smithfield district of Belfast, on the afternoon of Wednesday, 29 August 1832, when he killed his father, William Linn, in a brutal assault, during which he attacked him with a hatchet and stabbed him in the chest with a chisel.[4] Several months later, during the Co. Antrim assizes of March 1833, Linn stood trial for murder. A guilty verdict seemed inevitable – not least as Linn himself had made no attempt to conceal his guilt. Nevertheless, he escaped the hangman's rope. During the trial, evidence emerged that he had, 'for some time' prior to the assault, 'exhibited marks of derangement of mind' and the presiding judge intervened, advising the jury 'that there was abundant proof of the prisoner's insanity' and that they 'ought, at once, to return a verdict to that effect'.[5] This they did, and Linn was '[a]cquitted on the grounds of insanity' and placed, in due course, in the Belfast Lunatic Asylum, from which institution he was to escape in November 1835.[6] Following his escape, Linn remained at large for the best part of a year, and it was not until 1 September 1836 that he was recaptured, 'after a desperate resistance', in Dublin.[7] Detained initially in Dublin's Kilmainham gaol, Linn was later moved to Carrickfergus gaol in Co. Antrim, where his story would take a further turn.[8] Early in February 1838 a 'most daring and blood-thirsty conspiracy, on the part of the prisoners ... to murder the officers of the prison, and then effect their escape', was discovered – a conspiracy which appears to have been led by Linn.[9] Subsequently tried at the Co. Antrim assizes of March 1838, he was found guilty of administering unlawful oaths to fellow prisoners and sentenced to seven years' transportation.[10] Thus it was that John Linn came to be numbered among the 215 convicts who departed Dublin for New South Wales on board the *Clyde* in May 1838.

Combining, as it does, the ingredients of murder, madness, prison-breaking and transportation, Linn's story is a striking one. But it is also a story that has been overlooked. Although reported in detail by Belfast's newspapers, and discussed by contemporaries in a variety of contexts, it has attracted surprisingly little attention from historians.[11] Some twenty years ago, Keith Haines offered a partial account of Linn's story in an article published in the local history magazine *Due North* and the present author has, more recently, sketched the tale in brief in a contribution to Salvador Ryan's 2016 miscellany, *Death and the Irish*.[12] Necessarily limited in scope, these short articles constitute the fullest modern treatments of Linn's case.[13] Given this, one aim of the ensuing discussion is to offer a fuller and more carefully nuanced account of Linn's story, making use of the full range of extant source materials. In addition to the newspaper reports on which the existing accounts of Linn's story are principally based, these include the records of the Belfast Lunatic Asylum; two convict reference files, which include petitions from Linn to the lord lieutenant of Ireland and the detailed report of an investigation into the conspiracy discovered in Carrickfergus gaol in 1838; and, of particular value, an account of Linn's case that was published in the *Phrenological Journal* in 1836.[14] The latter is significant less for its author's attempted application of phrenology to Linn, than for its inclusion of a series of letters penned by John Grattan, a Belfast businessman with interests in phrenology and craniology who had 'carefully investigated' Linn, visiting him in the Belfast Lunatic Asylum and speaking with his sisters.[15] Taken together, these sources enable us to reconstruct Linn's story in detail. But beyond simply relating it, the chapters that follow will seek also to use Linn's story as a means to shed light on the society that produced and sought to deal with him. As such, the story of John Linn serves here as the basis for an exercise in microhistory, centring on the themes of crime and punishment.

First emerging in the 1970s and early 1980s, microhistory is best viewed, as Giovanni Levi has argued, not as a 'theory', but as a methodology or 'historiographical practice' that entails 'the reduction of the scale of observation' on the understanding that 'microscopic observation will reveal factors previously unobserved'.[16] To put this another way, we might say, quoting Gordon S. Wood, that microhistory 'takes small events in the past ... and teases out of them stories and meanings that presumably throw light on the larger society'.[17] The approach has not been without its critics. Indeed, Wood's subtle qualifier – 'presumably' – reflects his concern that the wider significance of microhistories is at times obscured by the novelty of the stories told: 'sometimes', he writes, 'the sheer intensity and interest of the particular stories overwhelm their larger significance, turning them into little trees in search of a forest.'[18] Nevertheless, the possibilities of microhistory have been established in seminal works by scholars such as Emmanuel Le Roy Ladurie, Carlo Ginzburg and Natalie Zemon Davis, and the approach is of particular value in cases – such as John Linn's – which involve crime and the courts.[19]

As Edward Muir and Guido Ruggiero have observed: '[a] crime is a moment when a culture fails in its own terms, a moment when microsystems challenge macrosystems of power and values'.[20] As such, the close study of criminal episodes and legal proceedings can offer glimpses of larger social dynamics. Thus while Muir and Ruggiero rightly warn that 'criminal records can never be simple windows into the past' and must be viewed as 'highly crafted images fashioned in accord with legal procedures', they also acknowledge that:

> the misdeeds of the past generated a body of texts that reveal otherwise unspoken cultural assumptions, that give voice to the illiterate, that disclose the discontinuities of the society, that generate little dramas about human conflicts and dilemmas, that resurrect the otherwise hidden life of the street ... and prison cell.[21]

As the following chapters will reveal, John Linn's misdeeds led to the production of sources through which we can explore contemporary attitudes and assumptions concerning a range of issues, including murder, insanity and imprisonment, and his story provides a point of entry into a society experiencing rapid social transformation and a community – the working class (or, more precisely, classes) of early 19th-century Belfast – that remains, in historiographical terms, relatively little known. Pursuing Linn's story not only takes us into the courtroom, the lunatic asylum and the county gaol, but reveals something of the 'hidden life of the street' and the drama, not always 'little', of familial tension and breakdown. If it is, above all, a story of crime and punishment, it is also a story that reveals the wider contexts – social, political and cultural – in which Linn's crimes were committed and his punishment administered.

1. 'A young man of ungovernable passions'

For the historian, John Linn is a frustrating figure. His story is an arresting one to be sure, but getting to grips with Linn himself presents difficulties. Particularly problematic is the fact that the vast bulk of the direct evidence relating to his life dates from the period 1832–8, during which the more sensational aspects of his story were unfolding. By contrast, evidence concerning his early years is limited. Linn is thus encountered in sources that were produced in response to, or underpinned by an awareness of, his crimes and misdemeanours. To put it bluntly, had Linn not killed his father in 1832 he would have left little trace in the historical record. Under such circumstances, penetrating his notoriety presents something of a challenge; in a sense, Linn the man is obscured by a construct – Linn the parricide, an infamous figure whose life is understood only in relation to its most shocking episode. This is not, of course, to deny that Linn was a parricide: he *did* kill his father. Rather it is to acknowledge that Linn led a life prior to killing his father, and to highlight the fact that the realities of his lived experience are concealed if we view him simply as a dangerous criminal deviant. With this in mind, we may begin our reconstruction of Linn's story by placing him in his particular social and cultural contexts, and by examining the fragmentary evidence that does relate to his early life. While there are, invariably, gaps in the story, it is nevertheless possible to piece together something of Linn's life in the years prior to his killing of his father. In so doing, we enter the world of Belfast's working class – a world of rapid urban expansion and confessional tension in which the one-dimensional figure of Linn the parricide is supplanted by that of Linn the Belfast 'hard man'.

* * *

Not least among the gaps in Linn's story is that concerning his date of birth. Two entries in the register of Dublin's Kilmainham gaol, where Linn spent time in 1836 and 1838, offer contradictory evidence. While the 1836 entry records Linn's age as 36, suggesting he was born in 1799 or 1800, the 1838 entry gives his age as 40, indicating that his birth occurred two years earlier, in 1797 or 1798.[1] This inconsistency is mirrored in two further records dating to 1838. Where an entry in a transportation register from that year gives Linn's age as 38, supporting the proposition that he was born in 1799 or 1800, a convict 'indent' created upon his arrival in New South Wales in September 1838 gives an age of 40, supporting an earlier date of birth.[2] The reason for this discrepancy is unclear, though it is by no means impossible that Linn was unaware of his precise date of birth and that the ages recorded in 1836 and 1838 were 'round' ages, selected for convenience. Whatever the case, the best that can be said regarding Linn's date of birth is that he was born at some point during the period 1797 to 1800. Also unclear is Linn's place of birth. While his convict 'indent' gives as a birthplace Co. Down, *where* in Co. Down he was born – whether in Belfast's immediate hinterland, or further afield – is not stated. Yet if basic biographical detail is limited, these scraps of information nevertheless suggest a plausible origin story for Linn: born in Co. Down *c.*1797–1800, he was most likely a rural in-migrant, brought to Belfast by his parents in the early years of the 19th century.

Migration of this nature was far from unusual. As is well known, Belfast grew rapidly in the late 18th and early 19th centuries. Between 1791 and 1831 the town's population rose from around 18,300 to over 53,200, as working people from the townlands of Antrim and Down abandoned the countryside in search of work in its warehouses, docks and growing textile mills.[3] During the same period, members of some of Belfast's better-known families appear to have quit the town: 'the numbers which have of late left it are really astonishing,' one Belfast woman remarked in 1802, 'of those too one would have supposed stationary, not a Hyde, one Greg, and no Cunningham, not a Holmes, Banks, or Black, or Wallace.'[4] Combined with the rapid population growth, this development dramatically changed the character of Belfast. A once close-knit town – a town that had, in the past, been 'based on face-to-face encounters', and whose earlier inhabitants had known the family backgrounds and histories of their fellow citizens – became, during the opening decades of the 19th century, a less personal and increasingly anonymous place.[5] It became a town with a large working class that needed to be employed, housed and – from the perspective of its middle-class social reformers – 'improved', a town with growing pockets of overcrowded and unsanitary housing and a town in which some fell through society's cracks, embracing criminality or joining the ranks of an immiserated, urban underclass.[6] It was in this rapidly changing urban community – a place both of opportunity and of peril – that John Linn would come of age.

The precise point at which the Linn family settled in Belfast is unknown, though John Linn's father, William Linn, can be placed in the town in the late 1810s. He appears in an 1819 Belfast directory, described as a 'wheelwright and turner', and it is likely that he had been resident in Belfast for some time prior to this.[7] Certainly, newspaper reports of his killing in 1832 suggest that he had a longstanding connection with the town. While the *Guardian and Constitutional Advocate* described William Linn as 'an old and respectable inhabitant', and made reference to his 'long residence' in Belfast, the *Belfast News-Letter* likewise noted that he was 'for many years a resident in this town'.[8] Read one way, such descriptions might appear to suggest that William Linn had settled in Belfast long before 1819, but given the backdrop of rapid population growth caution is required: what it in fact meant to be considered in the early 1830s as having been 'for many years a resident' in Belfast is, in reality, unclear. Intriguingly, other Linns are known to have been present in Belfast during the opening decade of the 19th century. A directory for 1807 lists a 'haberdasher and milliner' named Catherine Linn, an 'inn-keeper' named Patrick Linn and a 'spirit dealer' named David Linn, alongside a Robert Linn, of 'Robert Linn & co. soap-boilers and tallow-chandlers'.[9] Whether or not these individuals bore any relation to John Linn's family is unknown, though it is possible that they did and that the Linn family was drawn to Belfast by the 'pull' factor of extended familial connection.

* * *

Leaving aside the question of extended family, what of the immediate Linn family? Here, again, evidence is scarce. The identity of Linn's father is, of course, known, as also is his trade – as we have seen, William Linn was described as a 'wheelwright and turner'. By contrast, nothing is known of Linn's mother, though the fact that she is not mentioned at all in reports of William Linn's killing or John Linn's trial raises the possibility that she was, by the time of those events, deceased. Slightly more is known of Linn's siblings, of whom there were two: Rachel Catherine, who married Samuel Peel in May 1828, and Isabella Eliza, who was married to John Young, from Portglenone, in 1834.[10] Of the three Linn children, John Linn was the oldest by several years and it was later reported that 'his affection for his sisters was considerable'.[11] If there is a hint here of familial warmth, it should not be concluded that Linn's early life was an untroubled one, let alone a happy one. Although capable of displaying affection, Linn was also, in his sisters' telling, 'VERY *passionate*'. Indeed, they related that he 'had so little command over himself, that the most trifling provocation was sufficient to drive him into ungovernable rage' – and provocations there undoubtedly were.[12]

While much concerning Linn's early life is unclear, it is known that he had the misfortune to be born with a facial disfigurement in the form of a 'double hare-lip' – that is, a lip cleft in two places.[13] Early in his life, an attempt was made to repair the clefts.[14] This would have necessitated a painful and potentially traumatic operation. Common surgical practice when treating cleft lips in the early 19th century involved 'scarifying the margins of the cleft and suturing them together', though this procedure could have uneven outcomes.[15] Linn was left with a noticeable disfigurement and a speech impediment, and consequently acquired a cruel nickname. As the Belfast phrenologist John Grattan explained, while at school, Linn 'acquired the nickname of "Lippy Linn," which sobriquet has attached to him through life.' As a result, Grattan continued, 'he used to be continually engaged in boxing matches with his schoolfellows, until he became quite expert as a pugilist, and in consequence, when more advanced in life, became an amateur, attending prize-fights'.[16] We will return in due course to Linn's combative abilities, but at this point we may note that Grattan's claims regarding the longevity of Linn's cruel nickname are borne out in the columns of the *Belfast Commercial Chronicle*. Reporting the murder of William Linn early in September 1832, the paper noted that John Linn, who was, of course, the perpetrator, was 'better known by the appellation of *Lippy Linn*, from a remarkable disfiguration occasioned by harelip'.[17] Marked visibly as different, Linn was identified as such from an early age, receiving a moniker that proved as durable as it was unwelcome.

That Linn was first dubbed 'Lippy Linn' while at school raises the question of his education. There were, in early 19th-century Belfast, numerous opportunities to receive a schooling, from the rudimentary to the advanced. Under the heading 'Seminaries for Education, Teachers', Bradshaw's *Belfast general & commercial directory for 1819* lists 48 individuals. Alongside teachers in the Belfast Academy and the Academical Institution, the town's best-known schools, this number included a range of others, such as the 'Misses Knowles' of Donegall Street, Robert Hull of Castle Street, Monsieur Le Pan of Academy Street, Robert Pitts of Carrickfergus Street and Ann Ware of Chichester Street, who ran a 'seminary for young ladies'.[18] In addition, a range of charity and Sunday schools were established in the early years of the 19th century, providing educational opportunities for Belfast's ever-expanding working classes.[19] Where, precisely, John Linn received his education is unknown, though it is clear that he did receive one: his two surviving petitions to the lord lieutenant of Ireland testify to his ability to turn a phrase, and one contemporary, said to have known him 'intimately', asserted 'that he had been well "schooled," and could read and write'.[20]

Formal schooling aside, education of a different stripe was offered by church attendance. The Linn family can be identified as Presbyterian. While the marriage of Rachel Linn occurred by 'special licence' in St Anne's, the Church of Ireland parish church for Belfast, that of Isabella Linn took place in Third Belfast Presbyterian Church, and John Linn's convict 'indent' gives his religious affiliation as Presbyterian.[21] Insofar as it is possible to tell, the family's Presbyterianism was more than nominal. Certainly, William Linn was known to have been a devout man. At the time of his murder, Belfast's newspapers stressed his religiosity in terms that go far beyond the conventional blandishments we might expect to encounter in reports of such an event. Both the *Guardian and Constitutional Advocate* and the *Belfast News-Letter* informed their readers that he 'supported the character of an upright, honest man, distinguished by his kind and affectionate conduct as a member of society, and his unassuming piety and consistent walk as a Christian professor'. Both added, for good measure, that '[f]ew men in his situation attended more faithfully to the public and private duties of the Christian life than Mr. Linn', and the *Belfast Commercial Chronicle* likewise noted that he was 'described as having been most religious and exemplary all his life'.[22] The same could not be said for John Linn, but there is clear evidence that he was exposed to Presbyterian ministry, for speaking in 1825, in circumstances that will be discussed in due course, Linn stated that he attended 'Dr Hanna's meeting-house', Hanna being the Revd Samuel Hanna, the well-known minister of Third Belfast Presbyterian Church.[23]

First established in the 1720s by members of the longer-existing First and Second Belfast Presbyterian churches, who had become worried by the spread of 'lax views', Third Belfast was a theologically conservative congregation and Hanna, who was called to the church in 1799, was an 'impeccably orthodox' minister, whose preaching is said to have been 'remarkably evangelical'. Such details are significant insofar as they offer a glimpse into Linn's mental world: during the 1820s, when Ulster Presbyterianism was convulsed by theological dispute, Linn worshipped in a bastion of theological orthodoxy, under a minister who is known to have upheld the standards of the Westminster Confession of Faith.[24] Moreover, it appears from the accounts of those who encountered Linn during the period in which he was held in the Belfast Lunatic Asylum, that Hanna's ministry had a lasting impact upon him. It was later reported that Linn had, in a conversation with the asylum's 'Visiting Physician', Dr James M'Donnell, 'stated himself to be an orthodox presbyterian, and intimately acquainted with the tenets of that sect; indeed, he considered himself quite an expert theologian, and offered to discuss the merits of *the five articles* with any one.'[25] Whether or not M'Donnell availed of the opportunity to discuss the finer points of Presbyterian theology is unknown, but Linn's willingness to debate 'the five articles' – these being the Calvinist doctrinal fundamentals: 'total depravity', 'unconditional election', 'limited atonement', 'irresistible grace' and 'perseverance of the saints' – indicates that he had been doing rather more than day-dreaming when sitting under the ministry of Samuel Hanna.[26]

Worshipping in Third Belfast brought Linn within the orbit of one of Belfast's better-known families: the McCrackens. Representatives of the McCracken family, whose members included the social reformer Mary Ann McCracken and the United Irishman Henry Joy McCracken, are known to have retained a connection with Third Belfast until well into the 19th century.[27] However, as the son of a wheelwright Linn moved in rather different circles. While the McCrackens were a solidly middle-class family – albeit one whose members were, by the mid-1810s, less affluent than they had previously been – the Linn family was working class.[28] That being said, it is worth pausing to consider more carefully the Linns' social status. To state simply that the family was working class risks implying that the working class of early 19th-century Belfast was an undifferentiated mass. This was far from being the case. By the late 1830s, Belfast's workers were to be found in distilleries, breweries, glass and bottle making factories, iron foundries, brass foundries, tanneries and, of course, in textile mills, the biggest of which, S.K. Mulholland, Hind, a Co., boasted a workforce of 800. Added to this, there was porterage and labouring work on the docks – Belfast remained 'the mercantile capital for a large portion of Ulster' – and there were numerous opportunities for artisans and skilled craftsmen.[29] When the Belfast Mechanics Institute was established in 1825, its rules stipulated that 16 of its 24 directors were to be 'Operative Tradesmen' – that is, 'masters or journeymen, who actually work at their respective callings'. Revealing the breadth of skilled labour in the town, its first directors list included two founders (presumably foundry workers, rather than owners), two watchmakers and two machine-makers, alongside a tinsmith, a smith, a bookbinder, a carder, a confectioner, a chandler and an engraver.[30]

Belfast's working class was, then, a variegated community, and Linn's father occupied a distinctive place within it: he was, in short, respectable. As has already been noted, when the *Guardian and Constitutional Advocate* reported on the murder of William Linn, it observed that he was an 'old and respectable inhabitant of this town'.[31] In a similar vein, the *Belfast News-Letter* characterized him as 'a respectable old man'.[32] That William Linn was known to have been devout no doubt helped to inform such judgments. Religious commitment was closely linked with respectability and, in the Belfast context, particular concerns were being expressed about the large number of working-class Presbyterians who were unchurched; against this backdrop, religiosity served to set William Linn apart from the masses.[33] Equally important, however, was the nature of his work, and his economic status. As a wheelwright, William Linn was of the class of skilled worker for whom the industrial revolution is said to have brought the possibility of an improved standard of living. His trade carried at least a degree of cachet, setting him above the status of the factory worker, and he appears to have been comparatively well-off.[34] He not only owned his own business, employing an apprentice and a journeyman, but possessed sufficient means to set his son up in business.[35] Like his father, John Linn was a wheelwright and was said to be 'an excellent mechanic'. However, when he married – most likely in the late 1820s, though details are scarce – William Linn 'made over to him a small freehold property, which produced him a fair annual income for a person in his station, and established him in a spirit-shop'.[36]

Overall, the picture that emerges is that of a family that was, for a period at least, 'on the up'. Indeed, it is possible to detect evidence of social advancement, albeit of a modest kind, in the marriage of Linn's sister, Rachel Catherine, to Samuel Peel in May 1828. Notices of the wedding identify Peel as a 'grocer', indicating that Rachel Catherine climbed a rung on the ladder from working to middle class when she married.[37] It must be stressed, however, that there was a considerable distance to climb. For all the evidence of their (relative) prosperity, and whatever the descriptive shortcomings of the bald phrase 'working class', the Linn family remained a working-class family. William Linn may well have been skilled and respectable, but he was, nevertheless, a tradesman who worked with his hands. Moreover, while he may have possessed sufficient capital to set his son up with a freehold property, it does not follow that John Linn was possessed of the temperament or ability to take advantage of this and further climb the social ladder. Quite the reverse, as John Grattan later related, following a conversation with Linn's sisters, soon after his marriage Linn 'got into debt, sold his property, and in a very short time returned with his wife and children perfect paupers to the house of his father.'[38] In this sense, the story of the Linn family serves to remind us not only of the finely graded distinctions that existed within the working-class community of early 19th-century Belfast, but also of the potentially transitory nature of social mobility within that community: status and respectability earned by one generation could easily be lost by the next.

* * *

The house to which Linn returned – having squandered the resources his father provided him with – was located in the west of the town in Smithfield. One of the best-known working-class quarters of 19th-century Belfast, Smithfield was first developed in 1788, when a market was established in land lying between Millfield and Hercules Street, and had emerged, over time, as a distinctive and densely populated 'residential district'.[39] By 1823, Smithfield Square alone housed a population of 354 people in some 56 houses, while the population of the greater Smithfield area as a whole stood at over 3,000.[40] Included in this number were the Linn family. William Linn's entry in Bradshaw's 1819 Belfast directory gives his address as '38 Smithfield', and he appears to have remained in the quarter until the time of his death in 1832, for in its report of his killing the *Belfast News-Letter* placed William Linn in 'a house on the western side of Smithfield', noting that he had 'long resided' there.[41]

Glimpses of Smithfield as William Linn and his children would have known it can be found in two sources: Thomas Gaffikin's reminiscences of early 19th-century Belfast, written towards the end of the century; and *The 'Northern Athens'; or, life in the Emerald Isle*, an intriguing, anonymous poem published in Belfast in 1826. In Gaffikin's description, Smithfield appears as a bustling, boisterous quarter. 'On ordinary days', he conceded, 'Smithfield was a dull enough looking place'. But it presented 'a busy scene on fair and market days' and came to life on 'Friday evenings', when crowds gathered 'to witness the different spectacles and amusements provided by the grinning clowns at the show booths, and the recruiting parties playing the "British Grenadiers" with fife and drum'.[42] A similar sense of clamour and commotion is conveyed by the description of Smithfield and its 'motley wonders' that appears in *The 'Northern Athens'*, though the poem's author goes somewhat further, depicting a more explicitly disordered streetscape. With an undertow of drunkenness ('Poteen each heart to fire and fury swells') and violence ('Here PAT, with cudgel tuck'd beneath his arm, / Halloos, and pulls his SHEELAH thro' the throng'), Smithfield is depicted as a riotous, carnivalesque space – a world turned upside down, in which the normal rules of society did not always apply. Indeed, this latter point is made explicit, with an apt literary allusion:

> VANITY FAIR, of which John Bunyan tells,
> Ne'er equall'd jovial SMITHFIELD'S ranting sight,
> Where matchless Folly shakes his cap and bells.
> And every right is wrong, and wrong is right; – [43]

Some allowance should no doubt be made here for poetic licence – but only some, for as the 19th century progressed Smithfield acquired a reputation as a distinctly seedy and unsavoury district.[44] The judgment of the Revd W.M. O'Hanlon, who visited the district in 1852, serves neatly to illustrate the point: 'I should suppose', O'Hanlon observed of Smithfield, 'that the very worst grade of our population will be found heaped together, corrupting and being corrupted, in this quarter.'[45]

O'Hanlon's Smithfield was a district in which one could encounter 'explosions of brutality', 'the sounds of cursing and blasphemy' and 'moral deformity and odiousness', a district in which 'the elements of poverty, wretchedness, ignorance, immorality, and irreligiousness' could be found 'seething ... as in a mighty cauldron'.[46] This was not necessarily Smithfield as the Linns had known it. Evidence from the 1837 valuation of Belfast reveals the presence, in Smithfield, of a reasonable proportion of housing in the mid to upper valuation categories, suggesting that it was not, at that point, the festering sore of poverty and criminality that O'Hanlon would encounter in the early 1850s.[47] But there was also, as Stephen A. Royle has noted, 'a growing sector of low value housing' in the area, and if the Linn family might not have known Smithfield at its squalid worst there were, nevertheless, similarities between the Smithfield of the 1820s and that of the mid-century.[48] While O'Hanlon 'counted about twenty public houses' in the quarter when he visited in 1852, Gaffikin's account indicates that many of the 'dwellings' that surrounded Smithfield's central market square were, at an earlier point, 'occupied by publicans', and the violent scenes that characterized Smithfield in the 1850s – O'Hanlon wrote of 'fierce, and often bloody, struggles' – were not without precedent.[49]

One significant corollary of the population growth Belfast experienced in the early 19th century was the increase in size of its Catholic community. Writing in 1792, one visitor to Belfast had remarked of the town's population that '[v]ery few are papists & those of the very lowest class'.[50] By the 1830s, this situation had been transformed, if only numerically. The Catholic community had grown to comprise approximately a third of Belfast's population, and distinct Catholic enclaves had developed – enclaves including the Chapel Lane region in Smithfield, the site of Belfast's first Catholic chapel, opened in 1784, and Hercules Street, which marked the easterly boundary of the greater Smithfield quarter.[51] As a result, Smithfield and Hercules Street served, at times, as a stage on which violent confrontations between rival Catholic and Protestant, or 'Orange', mobs were played out and it is in accounts of one such confrontation – that which occurred on 12 July 1825 – that John Linn makes his first appearance in the historical record.[52]

* * *

The events of July 1825 were sparked by the determination of a group of Smithfield Orangemen to commemorate publicly the Battle of the Boyne and, in so doing, to 'hurl defiance' at the government's effective proscription of the Orange Order under the terms of the 1825 Suppression Act.[53] Although born of the roiling confessional and economic tensions of late 18th-century Co. Armagh, Orangeism had been a presence in Belfast from an early point.[54] Indeed, it was rumoured in March 1796 that 'an host of Orangemen were coming from the county Armagh' in order to 'destroy' the town. The anticipated 'host' did not, in the end, make an appearance, but in July 1797 Belfast did witness a 'formidable display' of Orange Order strength when 'upwards of 6,000' Orangemen gathered in the town and 'walked through the principal streets ... bearing orange flags'.[55] But if the Orange Order was an early presence in Belfast, it does not follow that it was universally approved. Writing after an Orange demonstration in July 1802, the Belfast-woman Martha McTier observed that the town's Orangemen had 'in ridiculous array paraded all the day before, to the no small disapprobation if not dismay of many of their former snug friends', adding that 'a very great number of green silk handkerchiefs' had been 'spitefully displayed'.[56]

Eleven years later, on 12 July 1813, a riot occurred and two were shot dead, following the return, from Lisburn, of a group of Belfast Orangemen, and further confrontations took place in the early 1820s.[57] Thus, on 11 July 1823, *The Irishman* printed a public 'caution' that had been issued by 'the Justices assembled at the general sessions of the peace, in Belfast'. Conscious that 'riotous and tumultuous mobs had assembled in the town of Belfast on the evenings of the 12 July, and following days, for several years past, and have proceeded to serious acts of violence, to the great disgrace of the town', the magistrates warned 'against the repetition of such outrages'. Their determination that individuals 'who may be hereafter convicted of Rioting, will be punished by *fine and imprisonment*' appears to have had the desired effect, and 12 July 1823 proved peaceful.[58] 'Not the slightest disturbance took place in the course of the day', the *Belfast News-Letter* subsequently reported, 'and the police office was never more clear of prisoners than on Saturday night.'[59]

As on 12 July 1823, peace prevailed on 12 July 1824: reporting that the day had 'passed over ... with perfect tranquillity', the *Belfast News-Letter* judged it 'the quietest 12th of July that has occurred for many years.'[60] Trouble was, however, to return in July 1825, when the twelfth was marked by displays of 'party animosity'.[61] Early in the day, it became clear 'that an Orange procession was preparing to celebrate, in Smithfield, the anniversary of the Battle of the Boyne.' When one of the Belfast magistrates, Mr Ferrar, attempted to dissuade the Smithfield Orangemen from pursuing this course, he was met with 'opprobrious epithets of contumely and abuse', and an unseemly squabble took place when he tried, unsuccessfully, to confiscate an 'Orange banner'. Matters deteriorated as the day progressed. As the *Northern Whig* put it, 'various fights took place between the contending parties. Missiles of every description were thrown, and … several persons were injured.'[62] These included 'a respectable looking young man and woman', who were 'wantonly assaulted by some ruffians' in Smithfield (one of 'the chief scenes of action'); 'a young man of 16', who was 'severely' beaten in Sandy Row; and John Linn, who was involved in a vicious brawl in High Street.[63]

These events were first reported on 14 July 1825 in the *Northern Whig*, which made a passing reference to a 'battle' having been 'fought in High Street, which lasted some time.'[64] On 15 July, however, the *Belfast News-Letter* published an 'authorized report' of the rioting, supplied by Belfast's police office. This included more details of the clash in High Street, and related Linn's story as follows:

> About three o'clock a young man named Linn, having bought some cloth at a shop in High-street, was proceeding peaceably home with the cloth under his arm, when he was surrounded by several men near the Donegall Arms, who beat him, knocked him down, and when down kicked him unmercifully, – Linn, though an Orangeman, had taken no part whatever in the proceedings of the day, being one of those whose allegiance was not spurious.[65]

As depicted here, Linn appears as an innocent victim of mob violence. An Orangeman, yes, but a respectable, law-abiding Orangeman who had not participated in illegal processions or rioting, and who had been violently assaulted while going peacefully about his business. However, the fact that Linn was *known* to have been an Orangeman raises the possibility that there was more to the assault upon him than might at first meet the eye. As will become clear, this was precisely the case.

In the aftermath of 12 July 1825 blame was, inevitably, apportioned. Belfast's magistrates – and Ferrar in particular – were reproached by the *Northern Whig* for their lack of 'firmness' and 'lamentably deficient' response when faced with Orangemen 'who openly determined to trample upon all law'; a handful of publicans were deprived of their licences 'in consequence of their having entertained Orange Lodges'; and over two dozen men were brought to the dock to answer charges of 'riotously assembling' – and, in some instances, of assault – at the Antrim assizes held towards the end of July 1825.[66] Ten of these men – Alex M'Allister, John M'Keown, John Carr, Charles Bradley, John M'Lean, Simon M'Anally, Pat M'Anally, John Magee, Robert Whiteman and Henry Magee – were tried for the attack on Linn, all bar one (Robert Whiteman) being found guilty and sentenced to a year's imprisonment.[67]

More significant than the outcome of the trial, however, is the nature of the evidence that was heard. First in the witness box was Linn himself, who testified that he had been on High Street 'about three o'clock' on 12 July, had witnessed 'an Orange Lodge coming down the street' and had been attacked when he intervened and attempted to 'protect' a 'little boy' who had attracted the attention of a violent 'mob'. Echoing the *Belfast News-Letter*'s earlier report of his assault, Linn presented himself as a law-abiding citizen who had been an innocent bystander on the afternoon in question. He '[h]ad not been walking with the Orangemen' – indeed he 'considered they were [act]ing very wrong in walking in opposition to the law' – and had only been drawn into a brawl when attempting to play the role of a Good Samaritan. He might, he conceded, have 'struck' a certain John M'Lean, for he 'struck all around when the mob commenced first', but he was a victim, not an aggressor: he had been 'knocked down', 'kicked' and 'stabbed under the eye' in an assault that left him 'confined a week in his bed'.[68]

As might be expected, the witnesses for the defence offered a different version of events, suggesting that Linn was not quite the innocent bystander he claimed to be. While a Mr Carruthers of Castle Street testified that he 'saw Linn strike some person' and that 'this was before he was struck himself', a William M'Sowerly related that he had observed Linn in Castle Street where 'he was beating Henry Magee', and that he 'then turned about and made a blow at M'Lean'. Whatever the nature of Linn's role in the fracas, two points emerge clearly from the evidence presented in court. First, it is apparent that he received a brutal beating. Linn's own evidence on this score was supported by that of two witnesses. James Brady testified that he had witnessed 'Linn lying on the ground' and observed John and Henry Magee 'jumping on him and kicking him', while the physician who had attended to Linn's injuries related that 'he appeared very much confused, and there was a wound under the eye as if given with a sharp instrument'. Secondly, it is clear that there was a pre-history to the brawl and that the violence directed towards Linn was far from being random. Linn himself testified that he 'heard the mob say – "Its Linn … down with him … kill him … they have no law to-day"'. Similar statements were alluded to by John Muldrew, who gave evidence to the effect that one of the defendants had instructed Linn's attackers to 'lay on as there was no law that day', and by John Brady, who claimed to have heard a voice saying 'it is Linn; kill him, kill him'.[69] From such evidence it appears that Linn's attackers were determined to take advantage of the generalized disorder of 12 July 1825 to harm him, and that it was *him*, in particular, that they wished to harm.

What accounts for this? The most obvious answer is that Linn was attacked because he was an Orangeman. That this was known has already been alluded to: in its report of his assault, the *Belfast News-Letter* noted that 'Linn, though an Orangeman, had taken no part whatever in the proceedings of the day'.[70] Linn, however, was no typical, rank-and-file member of the Orange Order, but a prominent Orangeman with a distinctive reputation. One aspect of this is illustrated by the anonymously authored 1826 poem, *The 'Northern Athens'*. At one point during its teasing, satirical survey of Belfast life, the poem's regular flow of eight-line stanzas breaks, and a poetic description of 'An Orange Dinner' is presented. Here, we encounter thinly veiled allusions to a number of evidently well-known Orangemen, including 'a good tallow chandler' of North Street; 'WHEELY', who 'Enunciated with a twang and a wh-wh-whistle'; and 'SLIPSLOP', 'a lisping orator' with a noticeable squint.[71] While the identities of these individuals are no longer known, the subject of the following passage is instantly recognizable:

> Another Patriot rose, who meant to tip
> A speech – a well-known Patriot with a *lip*;
> A gift of tongue kind Nature had bestow'd him,
> Which he could rattle if his lip allow'd him.
>
> Thus LIPPY:– 'Friends! The glorious Twelfth now past,
> May prove to Orange Privilege the last.
> O, by the gods! if aught inspire regret,
> It is, to find the Papists in our debt,
> Who, in Corn-market, dar'd our ranks to pelt –
> Our eyes beheld them, and our craniums felt –
> But, tables soon may turn – our daily prayer –
> Then let the knaves of Herc'les-street beware!
> Whose *Butcher* carcases shall find defeat,
> The vermin's hearts all rotten as their meat.'
> He ceas'd – as sometimes best declaimers may,
> Who have no more upon the point to say;
> Whilst the fir'd, anxious auditors await
> LIPPY in dumbness, as in high debate;
> Who drank 'The Pious Memory – may it shine
> In living lustre like the glorious BOYNE.'[72]

As satirized in *The 'Northern Athens'*, Linn appears as a 'well-known Patriot', an Orange speechifier who thundered against the 'Papists' of Belfast, stoking the flames of confessional resentment. To this picture, however, we can add the detail provided by John Grattan, who visited Linn in the Belfast Lunatic Asylum. As has been noted, Grattan highlighted Linn's skill with his fists: teased as a schoolboy, he explained, Linn resorted to fighing and 'became expert as a pugilist', so expert that as an adult he 'became an amateur, attending prize-fights'. But this was not the whole story. Given its growing confessional tensions, Belfast in the 1820s provided particular outlets for men with such skills, and Grattan had more to say about the contexts in which Linn engaged in combat. 'Possessed of great bodily strength and prowess,' he wrote of Linn, 'he then became the champion of the orangemen, of which society he was a member, being put forward upon all occasions to fight their battles and bully their opponents.'[73]

Not simply a ranting, anti-Catholic speech-maker, Linn was thus a well-known brawler. He was Belfast's Orange 'champion', and it is in this light that the events of 12 July 1825 should be viewed. Linn was attacked by a group of men who knew precisely who he was, and who, having spotted him in isolation, seized the opportunity to overcome his 'great bodily strength' – it was later said that he 'was usually able to prostrate six ordinary men without much difficulty' – and deprive Belfast's Orangemen of their defender.[74] Added to this, however, was the particular spice of personal resentment and rivalry, for one name recurs in the *Belfast News-Letter*'s report of the trial of Linn's attackers: M'Lean. During the course of the trial two M'Leans were referred to: John M'Lean, and his father James. The latter was not present in court in July 1825. He was said to have 'fled', and it was not until late in March 1826 that he was brought to trial, though at that point he was acquitted of assault.[75] His role in the events of 12 July 1825 was disputed: where Linn gave evidence to the effect that he had been restrained by James M'Lean 'while the others beat him', a defence witness at his trial in March 1826 painted him as a peacemaker, who had attempted 'to separate his son and Linn'.[76] By contrast, it is clear that John M'Lean was prominently involved in the attack on Linn. One witness at the trial in July 1825, Mary Dickson, testified that she saw him 'take a knife from his sleeve and go into the crowd', suggesting that it was he who stabbed Linn, and as the melee developed M'Lean and Linn engaged in a particular exchange of blows. It appears, moreover, that Linn was familiar with M'Lean. In court, under cross-examination, he revealed that he understood M'Lean to be 'an apostate' who was married to 'a Roman', and pointed out that 'he never saw him' at his own place of worship, which was, of course, 'Dr Hanna's meeting-house'.[77] In all of this, the outlines of a personal dispute and a rivalry driven by confessional tensions begin to emerge – outlines that are brought into focus by the recollections of Thomas Gaffikin, who recalled, later in the century, that M'Lean was to Belfast's Catholics what Linn was to its Orangemen – their 'champion'.[78] Whether the brawl of 12 July 1825 was Linn's first encounter with M'Lean, or one of a series of clashes that had begun earlier in the 1820s, cannot be said for certain. It is clear, however, that the attack on Linn formed part of a longer story of violent Catholic–Protestant interaction, and that Linn was a well-known Belfast personality well before he killed his father. Indeed, he appears, in a certain sense, as prototypical. Long after Linn's day, the idea of the Belfast 'hard man' would emerge, typified by Alexander Robinson, or, as he was better-known, 'Buck Alec'. A loyalist gunman during the turbulent 1920s, and later a noted street-fighter and Belfast 'character', famed for his pet lions, Robinson illustrates the process whereby violence provides 'a route to status for working-class men'.[79] But the Belfast hard men of the 20th century had their 19th-century predecessors, and Linn, the Orange 'champion' of the 1820s, has fair claim to the title of Belfast's first Protestant 'hard man'.

* * *

Several months on from the rioting and legal proceedings of July 1825, Linn made a further appearance in Belfast's newspapers when John M'Lean, who had evidently been released early from prison, accused him of intimidating behaviour. In M'Lean's telling, Linn had visited his home and had, while 'brandishing a hatchet', vowed to kill him 'and every papist that would meet him'.[80] Viewed – somewhat oddly, given the pair's history – as a petty crime, this case was heard in the sovereign's office late in February 1826, and the *Northern Whig*'s account of the proceedings offers an intriguing picture of Linn as he appeared to one contemporary:

> Defendant, a stout, well-dressed young man, with an impediment of speech occasioned by a hare-lip, in reply to the charge, asserted that he had been goaded almost to madness by complainer's party calling him *"lippy Linn;"* that the present complaint had been got up to prevent a prosecution, which would take place at next Assizes, against some of complainer's party; and concluded by vociferating that if Orangemen were not *righted*, they would not always submit to insult.[81]

The Irish court, Katie Barclay has recently argued, was a 'performative space' – a space in which 'men, and occasionally women, told stories to men with the aim of convincing them to believe their version of events or the law'.[82] What is striking in the *Northern Whig*'s clipped account of Linn's court appearance in February 1826 is the multiplicity of roles he played, and the variety of stories he told. That he is said to have been 'well-dressed' is by no means incidental, for clothes doubled as 'a quick measure of social value' and 'a respectable outfit was read as evidence of character.'[83] Outwardly, Linn thus played the part of a respectable young man. There was, of course, nothing respectable about the behaviour he was accused of, but he countered this with a two-pronged narrative of victimhood. On the one hand, he was a man with a speech impediment who 'had been goaded almost to madness by the complainer's party'; on the other, he was a victim of conspiracy. John M'Lean's father was due to stand trial at the forthcoming spring assizes for his role in the events of 12 July 1825; was his son's complaint not an attempt to 'prevent a prosecution'? This narrative of victimhood was, however, undermined by the final guise Linn adopted, that of a belligerent, threatening Protestant: 'if Orangemen were not *righted*,' he railed, 'they would not always submit to insult.' Victim and aggressor; quarrelsome Orangeman and young man with the wherewithal to present himself as respectable: Linn was all of these things – and more. Perhaps, though, he is best characterized in the words of the magistrate who heard his case in February 1826: unimpressed by Linn's 'ebullition of intemperance', he rebuked him 'for using such language', remarking that it 'clearly appeared that he was a young man of ungovernable passions'.[84] As the following chapter will reveal, these words proved prophetic.

2. 'Horrid Murder. – Parricide.'

In archival terms, John Linn recedes from view in the late 1820s. Towards the end of March 1826, just a few weeks after his own appearance in Belfast's sovereign's office, he stood as a witness during the belated trial of John M'Lean's father and two others – John M'Laughlin and John Wood – for their role in the events of the previous 12 July.[1] In the *Northern Whig's* account of this, his third court appearance, we encounter Linn once more as a belligerent figure, albeit one attempting to reconcile respect for the law with commitment to the principles of Orangeism: when 'closely questioned', it was reported, he 'emphatically remarked, that he had ceased mingling in the parades of Orangemen, purely in obedience to the laws of the country; but that he still maintained, and would continue to uphold their principles, *which every true Protestant in the country should feel bound firmly to stand by*.'[2] Thereafter, Linn slips into obscurity and little can be said for certain concerning his life during the six-year period that followed. It is likely, though, that he married during these years, for by 1832 he had a wife, Susannah Linn, and four daughters: Anna Isabella, Maria Caroline and Martha, who appear to have been born during the period 1826–9; and a fourth, whose name is unknown.[3] Likewise, it appears that he spent some time away from Belfast. Speaking in March 1833, Arthur Murphy, a journeyman who had worked with William Linn, described Linn's behaviour 'about nine or ten months before' when he was 'in Liverpool, at his work', suggesting that he had left Belfast in search of employment.[4] It is possible that he travelled with Murphy as a journeyman wheelwright. Certainly, he had the skills to do so. 'His mechanical abilities were so great', noted John Grattan, whose letters on Linn later appeared in an article in the *Phrenological Journal*, 'that his sister says when he has received new models, his own work has generally been superior to the original.'[5] The exact length of Linn's absence from Belfast is unknown, but he had returned to the town by late July 1832, and on 29 August 1832 he dramatically remerged from obscurity when he visited his father's Smithfield workshop and killed him.[6]

* * *

At around one in the afternoon on 29 August 1832, William Linn was in his workshop, 'stripped at work with his shirt sleeves tucked up'.[7] He was not alone: 'an old woman' was present, 'getting her wheel righted', while the journeyman,

Arthur Murphy, and an apprentice named William M'Gowan were also 'at work'.[8] Into this busy scene burst John Linn, seemingly accompanied by his wife and in an agitated state: he was, Murphy later testified, 'quite deranged looking' and 'foaming at the mouth'.[9] William Linn's heart might have sunk at the sight of his son, for relations between the two were troubled. Linn and his family had been living with him until shortly before 29 August 1832, but had recently moved out.[10] As the *Belfast News-Letter* explained, this led to a quarrel between the two men: '[F]or some time past, we understand, a difference had existed between him [Linn] and his father, in regard to several articles of property which he claimed on his removal with his wife and children to another house.' But the quarrel was not about property alone, for Linn's 'general habits and character had been so much the reverse of those of his father, that a cordial understanding between them did not exist, and could scarcely have been expected to exist.'[11] We have already seen something of Linn's 'habits and character'. As detailed in chapter one, he was a well-known brawler. Added to this, he appears also to have been given to drunkenness and fits of uncontrollable temper. John Grattan later reported that Linn had been 'much attached to his wife and children, except when under the influence of one of those "gusts of passion," or when excited by drink, to which he was addicted, having at one time kept a public house or spirit shop.'[12] Likewise, he noted that 'the most trifling provocation was sufficient to drive him into ungovernable rage', relating an example provided by Linn's sister:

> He was in bed, when, hearing his wife in altercation with a servant, she says his *breathing seemed absolutely to cease for a time*, after which, bounding upon the floor with terrific energy and a force which actually shook the room, he gave vent to his accumulated wrath in violent imprecations and threats against the servant, whose life she really believes he would have taken could he have caught her; though all the time he was entirely ignorant of the offence she had been guilty of and which was actually quite trifling.[13]

The reference, here, to a servant offers further indication that the Linn family, if working class, was comparatively well-off. More significant, however, is the fact that Linn's fury, on this occasion, was provoked by hearing his wife quarrelling with a servant, for Grattan's account would suggest that Linn's marriage had had a destabilizing impact on Linn and his family. 'Prior to his marriage, *which was one that did not please his family*', Grattan wrote, 'his affection for his sisters was considerable, and a calm look or quiet word from them would recall him to himself. But afterwards his attachment was transferred to his wife, of whom he was passionately fond.'[14] In the years following, relations within the Linn family deteriorated. As we have already seen, William Linn had set his son up in business when he married. In due course, however, Linn 'got into debt' and returned, poverty stricken, to the family home. It was at this point that the trouble began – or so Linn's sisters claimed. 'From this period', Grattan noted, 'the family date all their misfortunes':

> As being an only son, and the eldest child, he [Linn] seemed to consider himself entitled to every thing, and grudged every penny that was laid out on other members of the family … one of his sisters works most beautifully with her needle, and her father naturally felt pride in framing the pictures she worked for him and hanging them in his parlour; but his son, to whom he had been beyond measure liberal, considered this so unreasonably extravagant, that at last, to do away with the irritation and quarrels which they occasioned, the old man actually removed them from the room.[15]

The image of a framed, needle-work picture, removed from a wall to pacify a quarrelsome, avaricious son, given to drunkenness and outbursts of violence, is an evocative one, suggestive of domestic disharmony and strained bonds of affection. It may even, on balance, be a largely accurate one. Nevertheless, a degree of caution is required here. That Grattan's account of the Linn family's tribulations was based on information received from Linn's sisters gives pause for thought, for he also noted Linn's claim that it was thanks to the influence of one of his sisters that a rift had opened between him and his father.[16] In short, we should not assume that Grattan had access to the whole story. Nor, moreover, should we seize uncritically on the suggestion that the family's domestic happiness was shattered by Linn's marriage, for this comes close to attributing blame for the whole affair to a figure – Linn's wife – who is entirely voiceless, and largely invisible, in the surviving sources.

Whatever might be said about its character, it is clear that the quarrel within the Linn family entailed more than petty jealousies and minor resentments. Indeed, Linn's relationship with his father had turned violent prior to the events of 29 August 1832. In its report of William Linn's killing, the *Guardian and Constitutional Advocate* included an intriguing reference to an earlier incident, said to have occurred '[a] few weeks ago', during which Linn had been 'sent to gaol for a violent assault on his father'.[17] No mention was made of this in the reports that appeared in the *Northern Whig*, the *Belfast News-Letter* or the *Belfast Commercial Chronicle*, but a statement penned several years later by the governor of Carrickfergus gaol, James Erskine, confirms that Linn had been 'committed to the County Antrim Gaol for an assault on his Father the 27th July [and] discharged on bail the 6th August 1832'.[18] Moreover, when giving evidence at his trial for murder in March 1833, Linn's sister, Rachel Catherine Peel, referred to an episode that had occurred 'the Saturday before her father was killed', during which Linn had threatened to 'murder them all' and she had been obliged to fetch the police.[19] Clearly, the Linn family was a family in crisis, and when John Linn entered his father's workshop on 29 August 1832 he did

so with a considerable amount of baggage. Faced with his son, William Linn
no doubt anticipated another round in this ongoing quarrel. He might even
have anticipated another violent confrontation; Linn was, after all, in 'a very
wild state'.[20] But he could not have foreseen quite how violent things would
become. Upon entering the workshop, which is described as having been 'above
stairs', John Linn 'stood a little', before asking 'for his hammer and tools'. His
father responded that he 'had none belonging to him', at which point events
took a bizarre turn.[21] Linn 'lifted a cage containing a bird', and made to leave
with it, claiming that 'he had bought seed for it'. His father 'calmly' objected,
pointing out 'that the bird and cage had been purchased by himself'. He offered
to reimburse Linn 'the three pence which he had expended, and desired him
to leave the bird.' At this point, Linn snapped and 'in a fit of frenzy jumped
upon the cage, which he smashed to atoms, bird and all'. Ominously, he then
'snatched up a hatchet'. The woman, for whom William Linn had been righting
a wheel, 'fled down the stairs', thinking 'he was about to strike her', but it was
towards his father that he directed his anger, slashing at him with the hatchet.[22]
Struck on the arm, William Linn 'reeled towards a bench', and at this point
Arthur Murphy and William M'Gowan 'ran down the stairs and proceeded
to the court-house for assistance'.[23] Linn's wife remained and 'struggled with
him to keep him from doing mischief'.[24] But to no avail. Having first attacked
his father with a hatchet, Linn then stabbed him with a chisel, killing him,
following which he 'proceeded to break the windows, and to destroy with the
hatchet every article of furniture in the house'.[25]

* * *

Linn's attack on his father was a brutal one. But how was it viewed at the time,
and how was Linn dealt with? Or, to put this another way, how did society
go about the business of reaffirming the standards of behaviour and the
'macrosystems of power and values' that Linn's actions had so dramatically
violated?[26] Beginning with the first of these questions, it is clear that Linn's
attack on his father was viewed with shock and horror. Thus the *Belfast News-
Letter* informed its readers that 'the neighbourhood of Smithfield … was thrown
into a state of agitation and horror' by the killing, while the *Belfast Commercial
Chronicle*, likewise, reported that 'a great degree of horror and dismay was
manifested in the neighbourhood of Smithfield' when it was first rumoured that
Linn had killed his father, and that it had transpired 'that the dreadful rumour
was but too true'.[27] In a sense, of course, expressions of shock and horror are to
be expected: murder is, by its nature, a shocking crime. However, in considering
the way in which the killing of William Linn was viewed some context is
required. The killing did not take place in a social and cultural vacuum, and it is
worth pausing to consider the question as to how unusual murder and violent

crime actually was in Ireland – and more specifically in Belfast – in the first half of the 19th century.

While many contemporary – and some more recent – commentators have portrayed 19th-century Ireland as endemically violent, Richard Mc Mahon's work has substantially modified this picture. Although conceding that Ireland was violent 'at certain times and in certain areas', Mc Mahon demonstrates, from a painstaking analysis of homicide figures deriving from the 1830s and 1840s, that it was not invariably so: levels of homicide, he argues, 'were not much greater than those found in nineteenth-century England and, in the present day, in Ireland, north and south', and in the first half of the 19th century Ireland was, on the whole, 'a society in which the use of violence was contained and controlled and in which violence was not central to the regulation of social, cultural or economic life'.[28] This appears to have been particularly true of Ulster, in every county of which homicide rates fell below the national average during the period 1831–50, and which Mc Mahon characterizes as 'probably the area of the country least prone to homicide in the first half of the nineteenth century'.[29]

But what of the growing city in the east of the province? If homicide was far from being a common or everyday occurrence in Ulster, it should not be concluded that the people of Belfast were innocents, wholly unfamiliar with murder or violent crime. As we have already seen from the treatment John Linn received in July 1825, when he was punched, kicked and stabbed under the eye, confessional riots had the potential to produce scenes of outrageous violence on the town's streets. Here, however, it is worth noting that the violent scenes that occurred in July 1825 were far from unique. In December 1832, the chairing of successful candidates following a parliamentary election precipitated a riot in Hercules Street, during which a man named James Warnock 'got his eye knocked out, his ribs broken and his arm fractured' and a John M'Aleavy, who was later sentenced to seven years' transportation for his part in the attack, 'drew a knife and cut him in the face, in the lip and under the eye'.[30] Savage as his treatment was, Warnock might, in the end, have counted himself lucky, for four were killed when the authorities resorted to firearms in an attempt to suppress the riot.[31] Likewise, as was noted in chapter one, two were shot dead during the riot of 12 July 1813, though on that occasion the guns were fired not by figures of authority, attempting to uphold law and order, but by members of the Orange Order, two of whom were subsequently found guilty of manslaughter.[32]

Rioting was not, though, the only context in which violent acts occurred. In April 1832, as Catherine Hirst has detailed, a man was stabbed and killed when he turned down a challenge to fight a group of five men in Millfield. In this episode, sectarianism clearly played a role: the victim was a Catholic, the man who stabbed him was a Protestant and the incident took place just a day after an Orangeman (Samuel M'Briars) had been killed by a group of men in Belfast's southern hinterland.[33] By contrast, motives of a different kind were on display in November 1828, when a would-be assassin, one James Willis, levelled a pistol at a cabinetmaker named Hugh Eccles, in Great Patrick Street. Willis appears to have been acting on behalf of a combination of journeymen, enraged by the obduracy Eccles had displayed in refusing to accept the terms they sought 'to impose upon their employers', though his plan was frustrated – and serious injury avoided – when his pistol misfired.[34] To these examples we may add that of Antonio de Silva, a Portuguese sailor sent to the gallows in August 1810 for the murder, the previous Easter, of Robert Morrison, a ship's carpenter, who had died from a stab-wound received in a confrontation that occurred outside a quayside drinking house.[35] And what are we to make of the *Belfast News-Letter*'s reference, in its report of the aforementioned killing of Samuel M'Briars in April 1832, to the 'nocturnal outrages which have been occurring lately' – outrages conducted by individuals who had taken to 'fastening leaden balls to the ends of short pieces of rope, which can be easily concealed inside the sleeve of a man's coat' – or of the *Guardian and Constitutional Advocate*'s report, just days after the killing of William Linn, that two men had been 'attacked by a set of unprincipled ruffians' and 'severely injured' while 'passing quietly and inoffensively through Smithfield'?[36]

From this dismal, and by no means comprehensive, litany of murder, attempted murder and assault, it appears that violent acts, both lethal and otherwise, were by no means unheard of in Belfast. But for all this, it is clear that the killing of William Linn was viewed with particular revulsion. The *Belfast News-Letter* went so far as to describe it as a 'diabolical act', and observed that it 'was attended with circumstances of peculiar atrocity' – sentiments echoed by the *Guardian and Constitutional Advocate*, which informed its readers that '[t]he circumstances are truly revolting'.[37] We need not look far in accounting for this particular sense of shock and revulsion, for the plain fact is that the killing *was* an event of 'peculiar atrocity'. As we have seen, John Linn made use of the tools that came immediately to hand, striking his father with a hatchet and stabbing him with a chisel. William Linn's body was later discovered surrounded by 'a great quantity of clotted blood', and the injuries identified by the surgeons who examined his body testify with grim eloquence to the frenzied and brutal nature of his killing:

> The principal wound was one on the left breast, apparently inflicted with a flat chisel, which had penetrated the cartilaginous part of the ribs, passed through the lungs, and divided two of the large arteries near the heart. Instant death must have been the consequence of such a wound. There were also two wounds on the left arm, apparently from the same weapon; also, a cut on the shoulder, as if from the blow of a hatchet.[38]

If death was sudden, William Linn nevertheless breathed his last fending off a hail of 'desperate blows'.[39] Unleashed on an unsuspecting victim, in a place of work, such extreme violence was not comprehensible in the way that other, more common, manifestations of violence were. Drunken brawls and party riots might have been deplorable, but they could, at least, be understood; the very brutal killing of an individual who was identified several times in newspaper reports as an 'old man' was something else entirely.[40] But if the sheer level of violence inflicted upon William Linn was in itself sufficient to render his killing particularly shocking, there was an additional factor contributing to the horror of the event – that of the relationship between victim and perpetrator. William Linn was, of course, John Linn's father, and what the citizens of Belfast were forced to confront in August 1832 was not simply a case of murder, but a case of parricide.

* * *

That the citizens of Belfast *were* forced to confront William Linn's killing as a parricide is clear from the headlines that appeared in the town's newspapers. Breaking the story on 30 August 1832, the *Northern Whig* printed an account of the killing under the blunt headline 'PATRICIDE'.[41] A day later, the *Guardian and Constitutional Advocate* was equally blunt, heading its report 'PARRICIDE', while the *Belfast News-Letter*'s coverage of the killing carried the title 'HORRID MURDER. – PARRICIDE.'[42] By contrast, the *Belfast Commercial Chronicle*'s headline – 'HORRID MURDER' – made no reference to parricide, though by the time its report appeared, on 1 September 1832, this was scarcely necessary.[43]

Headlines aside, particular reference to the parricidal nature of the killing was also made in the body of the reports that appeared in the *Northern Whig* and the *Guardian and Constitutional Advocate*. 'Yesterday,' the *Northern Whig* observed, 'one of the most revolting acts was perpetrated, in this town, which it has ever been our duty to record. A person, named Linn, who resided in Smithfield, was murdered by his son.'[44] Likewise, the *Guardian and Constitutional Advocate* opened its report by referring to the fact that the victim 'was killed by his own son', and later observed that John Linn would face 'a charge of parricide – a crime, fortunately of very rare occurrence in this part of the country'.[45] A distinctly conservative newspaper, the *Guardian and Constitutional Advocate* was here making a political point: 'this part of the country' was, of course, the north-east, and a binary was being established, albeit implicitly, between a law-abiding Ulster and a lawless south, where parricide was more common.[46] The reality, however, is that parricide, if by no means unheard of, was relatively rare throughout Ireland. Indeed, in his *Homicide in pre-Famine and Famine Ireland*, Mc Mahon has observed that the evidence is sufficient to 'suggest that parricide was less common in pre-Famine and Famine Ireland than in some jurisdictions in the present day.'[47]

Scholars working on parricide in early-modern England, Scotland and Wales have argued that it was considered to be an almost unthinkable transgressive act. Anne-Marie Kilday has suggested that parricide was 'something of a "taboo crime" north of the Tweed'. 'It was', she writes, 'an offence that was so unpalatable and so unacceptable to both individuals and to Scottish society more broadly, that it was only very rarely conceived of and seldom resorted to'.[48] Likewise, writing of England and Wales, Garthine Walker has identified parricide as 'an unimaginable crime', noting that it was 'condemned as so unnatural an act that it was scarcely comprehensible'.[49] That parricide was considered a 'taboo crime' in early 19th-century Belfast is readily apparent from the language the town's newspapers employed when reporting on the killing of William Linn: as has already been noted, the parricidal murder was described as 'one of the most revolting acts ... perpetrated, in this town' and identified as a crime 'of very rare occurrence'. But if parricide was a 'taboo crime' it was not a crime that was unheard of or unconsidered, for during the 1810s and 1820s the *Belfast News-Letter* had brought a number of parricide cases before its readers' attention. Several of these were French cases. Just a few years after the killing of William Linn, France produced arguably the best-known parricide of the early 19th century, in the figure of Pierre Rivière who, to use his own term, 'slaughtered' his mother and two siblings in Aunay in June 1835, and subsequently produced a memoir, publicized by Michel Foucault and a group of collaborators in the 1970s, in which he attempted to 'make known the motives which led me to this deed'.[50] Rivière's case appears not to have made it into the columns of the *Belfast News-Letter*, but a number of other, earlier cases did. In February 1811, for example, the *News-Letter*'s readers encountered the story of 'a most horrible murder' which had taken place the previous December in the Commune of Biozart: a woman named Madelaine Albert had, it was reported, killed her mother and father with an axe and thrown her youngest sibling, a three-year-old sister, down a well.[51] Likewise, the story of a woman who had been found guilty of 'horrible parricide' in Lot was reported in 1817, and 1824 brought news of Barbe Rose Chatelet, who killed her father with a pistol in Dugny; a woman from Charente of the name of Gauthier, who had conspired with her husband to poison her father; and Luis Vigny of Mailet in Gand, who murdered his mother 'with a knife', and who was sentenced to 'have his right hand cut off, and be immediately put to death'.[52] Although short, such reports nevertheless drew the idea of parricide to readers' attention, marking it out as a crime peculiarly horrible and worthy of note.

Opportunities to reflect on parricide were also provided by accounts of parricidal killings that had occurred in England, Scotland and Wales. These included the case of James Cheeseborough of Grange Moor in Yorkshire, whose killing of his mother following a dispute over some tobacco, 'a thing he was passionately fond of', was reported in January 1818, and the particularly shocking case of Jane Scott, who was sentenced to death in Lancaster in 1828 for killing her mother, and who confessed, before her execution, that she was also responsible for the death of her father, her niece and 'her own illegitimate child'.[53] Irish cases, too, were reported: late in January 1828 the *News-Letter* related that an inquest 'on the body of a smith of the name of Dwyer, an inhabitant of Cashel' had produced 'a verdict of wilful murder ... against the son of [the] deceased'.[54] But the parricide case that received most attention from the *News-Letter* was one that had occurred much closer to home, at Churchtumbler in Co. Antrim.

The Churchtumbler case involved two brothers, Robert and John Greer, who were found guilty of the murder of their father, Archibald Greer, in March 1817. The father's body had been discovered the previous April 'in one of his own out-houses ... mangled in a most shocking manner, and a hatchet lying near it', and the *News-Letter* reported on his sons' trial 'very copiously', noting that it had 'excited great interest in the public mind'.[55] That this should have been so is scarcely surprising. On the one hand, the case involved a well-connected and ostensibly respectable family: the victim, Archibald Greer, was a 'tythe proctor' and the 'brother of the Rev. Mr Greer, of Rasharkin', while John Greer, one of the two accused, was 'a clergyman, and was in the habit of teaching in families in the neighbourhood'.[56] Added to this, however, was the protracted nature of the case and the excitement of the trial itself. The Greer brothers should have been tried during the summer assizes of 1816, but their day in court was postponed 'on the ground of non-attendance of witnesses'. At the spring assizes of March 1817 a second attempt was made to postpone the trial, with the two brothers claiming that they had been 'closely and separately confined, without being allowed to have any communication with their friends; and that thus they were deprived of the means of preparing for their trial.' The judge, Baron M'Clelland, disagreed: 'concluding that the reasons assigned for postponing the trial were by no means sufficient', he proceeded – no doubt to the satisfaction of the large crowd that had gathered in the courtroom. As the eight-hour trial progressed, the crowd's patience was rewarded by moments of high drama: one witness who had been present when Archibald Greer was murdered described the killing in vivid detail, confessing under cross examination that he had 'earlier said that he knew nothing of the murder' and had produced 'evasive accounts as I did not like to be the means of prosecuting to conviction'; towards the end of the trial, as the judge was summing up and charging the jury, a hitherto absent witness entered the courtroom dramatically; and the proceedings drew to a close with the judge reaching for the black cap and, 'in a most solemn and impressive manner', sentencing Robert and John Greer to death.[57] Two days later, the pair were 'launched into eternity': John, the clergyman, maintained his innocence to the end, declaring from the gallows that '*I forgive my persecutors, prosecutors, and all my enemies, and I hope God will forgive them as I do*', while Robert urged him to confess and acknowledged himself to be '*a guilty sinner*'. The former died violently, the latter quietly: as the *Belfast News-Letter*'s account of the execution put it, 'Robert appeared to suffer little, but John was long convulsed'.[58]

Just as reports of parricidal killings in distant locations appeared in the columns of the *Belfast News-Letter*, so news of the Greer parricide was published elsewhere. Accounts of varying length appeared in the *Newry Magazine*, *Blackwood's Edinburgh Review* and the *Anti-Jacobin Review*.[59] The latter, edited by the 'arch-tory' John Gifford, who had earlier published 'exposés of the Irish uprising of 1798', viewed the Greer case as illustrative of Irish barbarity.[60] Following a two-part account, drawn largely from the *Belfast News-Letter*, it observed that the details of the case had been '*inserted to prove to our readers, the dreadful indifference with which Murder is regarded in Ireland; and the absolute necessity of restraining such a barbarous population by the strongest means*'.[61] What, one wonders, did the editor of the *Belfast News-Letter* make of this polemical use of his paper's report? Of rather more interest than its display of Hibernophobia, however, was the *Anti-Jacobin Review*'s publication of what it described as an '*original Letter ... written by John Greer after his commitment to prison*'. Protesting his innocence, Greer complained bitterly that the 'paroxysms of misery' he experienced as a result of his father's 'unnatural death' were exacerbated by the discovery that he was accused of the crime – 'a crime, the perpetration of which would stigmatize the very lowest of the brute creation ... the most heinous of all crimes, a crime worse even than that of Cain ... and considered as the very detestation of humanity'.[62] Whatever might be said of Greer's sincerity – he was, after all, found guilty – his florid description of parricide, a description no doubt calculated to appeal to the sensibilities of his correspondent, offers perhaps the clearest evidence of the way in which the 'taboo crime' was conceived of in early 19th-century Ulster.

* * *

By the early 1830s, then, the people of Belfast were not unfamiliar with the 'horrible crime of parricide'.[63] If the act itself was rare, a succession of newspaper reports, and the Greer case of 1816–17, had nevertheless provided a frame of reference, marking parricide out as particularly reprehensible. But John Linn's killing of his father was not simply an event to be thought about and categorized. It was also, more fundamentally, a criminal act that required a legal response; Linn had to be brought before a judge, and held to account. Before this could happen, however, he had to be detained, and the process by which he was apprehended and brought to trial offers a vivid glimpse of the enforcement of law and order in early 19th-century Belfast.

As we saw earlier, when Linn began his attack on his father Arthur Murphy and William M'Gowan, William Linn's journeyman and apprentice, ran to Belfast's courthouse in search of help. At this point, the court was accommodated in the recently constructed House of Correction, 'a dark, strong building of brick, surrounded by a high wall'. Located some distance to the south of Smithfield, the complex combined 'numerous cells and

apartments for the confinement or reformation of convicts', 'a small chapel
... where divine service is regularly performed' and 'a spacious hall ... for
the Quarter Sessions, in which the sovereign's and seneschal's courts are also
held'; appropriately enough, the building's entrance bore the gloomy legend:
'Within Amend, Without Beware'.[64] When Murphy and M'Gowan arrived
with news of the events unfolding in Smithfield 'the Magistrates were sitting,
and the Sovereign [Sir Stephen May] immediately desired a party of police
to proceed to the spot.'[65] The 'police' in this context was not the Royal Irish
Constabulary (RIC), but Belfast's municipal police force, which had come into
existence as a result of the 1816 'Belfast police act'; RIC officers were posted to
the town from the mid-1820s, but it was the municipal force, as Brian Griffin has
observed, that carried out 'the bulk of the police work in the fifty years from
1816 to 1865'.[66] By the early 1830s, this force comprised both night watchmen
and day constables, and was overseen by Cortland MacGregor Skinner, a justice
of the peace who had become superintendent of the police in January 1827,
following the death of W.H. Ferrar, who we have already encountered as the
subject of criticism concerning his mishandling of the events of 12 July 1825.[67]
Skinner himself would face criticism: in 1835, by which time he had given up
the superintendence, the commissioners of the inquiry into Irish municipal
corporations noted that his 'incompetence for the office' had been 'much
observed upon'.[68] This may have been so, but on the afternoon of 29 August
1832 he acted with despatch. Seemingly present when Murphy and M'Gowan
made their dramatic appearance at the courthouse, he proceeded to William
Linn's property in Smithfield, accompanied by a number of others, including
Murphy and M'Gowan, a police officer named John Dickson and the 'Town
serjeant', William Walker.[69] Upon arrival, the men discovered that the front
entrance was 'bolted'.[70] A blacksmith named John Heyland was 'asked to pick
the lock', but before he could do so the door was opened from the inside by
Walker, who had climbed a wall at the rear of the property and 'forced in the
back door'.[71] Skinner and a number of others then entered the property and,
having climbed the staircase to the workshop, discovered William Linn, 'lying
on his face, weltering in his blood, and quite dead.'[72]

But what of John Linn? When Skinner and the police officers had first
arrived at William Linn's house, John Linn was inside, destroying its contents:
John Dickson testified that he had, upon arrival at the property, 'heard a great
wreaking in the inside of the house'.[73] However, by the time Skinner and the
others had gained admittance Linn had departed, taking up a position on the
top of a wall located at the rear of the building. Armed with a hatchet and a
brickbat, he was initially reluctant to give himself over to the authorities. When
a man named Faithful Tate made the mistake of approaching his position, Linn
launched a brick at him, hitting him with such force that he had to be 'carried
home in a state of insensibility', and 'when desired to surrender ... he for some
time refused ... declaring that he had stabbed his father, and they might shoot

him if they pleased, that he would rather die honourably than be hanged'.[74] Evidently, he was well aware of the gravity of his crime, but in due course he was talked down from the wall, following which he was taken to the police office – a decidedly shabby building, located a short distance to the east of Smithfield, in Rosemary Street – where he appeared before Belfast's magistrates.[75] As W.E. Vaughan has remarked, in a forensic treatment of the working of murder trials in 19th-century Ireland, 'varying degrees of silence' were 'imposed' on those caught in the machinery of the law. Suspects and defendants:

> spoke before the coroner if they wanted to and if he allowed them to; they spoke to policemen and to the magistrates if they wanted to, but only after they had been warned not to; at their trial at the assizes, they did not speak at all, although they could speak after they were convicted and before they were sentenced.[76]

In Belfast's police office, Linn decided to speak. Accounts concerning his conduct vary. Where the *Belfast News-Letter* and the *Northern Whig* suggest that he appeared 'indifferent', the *Guardian and Constitutional Advocate*'s report suggests that he had displayed some remorse, claiming that 'he was sorry for what he had done'.[77] What is clear, however, is that he acknowledged that he had killed his father. As the *Belfast Commercial Chronicle* put it, he had, in front of the magistrates, 'freely admitted having taken his father's life'.[78]

There was, then, no mystery to the events of 29 August. Nevertheless, certain investigative formalities took place. The following day, two surgeons – Wales and Arrott – examined William Linn's body, and an inquest into his death was held. This most likely took place in Smithfield, possibly in Linn's house, or in one of the numerous nearby drinking houses, for it was standard practice for inquests to be held close to the site of the body's discovery.[79] Wales and Arrott gave evidence, as also did Arthur Murphy, William M'Gowan, John Heyland, John Dickson and a number of others, whose names are not given. Following a 'short deliberation', the coroner's jury arrived at a verdict: William Linn 'came by his death, in consequence, of a stab in the side, inflicted by his son, John Linn'.[80] At this point, the coroner's work was done. Although vested with the power to send suspects to trial, he was not on this occasion required to act, for the previous evening, following his appearance before the magistrates, Linn had been 'sent off under an escort to Carrickfergus gaol, fully committed to take his trial at the next Assizes'.[81] Thus, within a matter of hours, the police, magistrates and coroner of Belfast had dealt with the killing of William Linn, swiftly apprehending and processing John Linn, and passing him up the system to await the assizes, which dealt with such crimes as murder.[82]

'The assizes were', Vaughan has observed, 'busy affairs, especially in the 1830s.'[83] The Co. Antrim assizes of spring 1833 were no exception. They began late, at around four o'clock on the afternoon of 12 March 1833, the judges having been delayed thanks 'to the press of business in Armagh'. In his opening address to the grand jury, Chief Justice Charles Kendal Bushe expressed his regret at this, 'more especially as they would probably be fully occupied with what would come before them.'[84] His prediction proved accurate. In the days that followed, cases were heard involving theft of various kinds, murders, assaults, rioting and 'uttering a base sovereign', and at least one case – a libel case involving F.D. Finlay, editor of the *Northern Whig* – had to be 'postponed … in consequence of the quantity of business still remaining unfinished.'[85] Linn's case was heard on 16 March 1833, and is chiefly of note because of its verdict.[86] According to the accounts that appeared in the *Belfast News-Letter*, he was 'indicted for the wilful murder of Wm. Linn, his father, at Belfast, on the 29th August last, by giving him a mortal wound with a chisel in the left breast.'[87] Had Linn been found guilty and sentenced to death it would scarcely have been surprising: he had, after all, been seen attacking his father, and had confessed more than once to his murder. Moreover, he was a man with a known propensity for violence, who had earlier appeared before the authorities and been bound over to keep the peace in 1826.[88] Nevertheless, when brought to trial he escaped execution. Indeed, he was judged not guilty. Summarizing the case in 1838, the *Eighth annual report* of the Belfast Lunatic Asylum – an institution whose story had intersected, troublingly, with Linn's – explained that '[t]he defence set up was, that he was insane; which, being credited by the Jury, he was accordingly acquitted; and, as a matter of course, forthwith transmitted to this Asylum'.[89] In actual fact, things were more complicated: according to the *Northern Whig*'s account of Linn's trial, which appeared on 18 March 1833, the jury found him innocent when they were advised to do so by Chief Justice Bushe.[90] Subsequent accounts of the trial, published in the *Belfast News-Letter* and the *Guardian and Constitutional Advocate* on 19 March, omit this detail, but all three newspaper reports are in agreement concerning the reasons for Linn's acquittal: he was considered, in the words of the *Northern Whig*, to have been 'insane at the time of committing the offence'.[91]

The possibility that Linn was insane when he killed his father had first been mooted the previous August, in the initial reports of the murder. 'The whole affair is quite inexplicable,' the *Northern Whig* had concluded, on 30 August 1832, 'except on the supposition of insanity.'[92] A day later, the *News-Letter* adopted a similar line. 'The affair is almost unaccountable', it reasoned, 'on any other supposition than that the wretch [i.e., John Linn] was insane in consequence of his dissipated habits.'[93] The casual invocation of insanity in these passages is intriguing, for Linn's case occurred at a time when the concept of criminal insanity was somewhat hazy. 'The idea that a defendant's criminal insanity mitigates his guilt has an ancient history in the common law', Catherine L. Evans has remarked. 'But the story of criminal insanity in Britain and the wider common law world as we now know it begins in earnest at the turn of the 19th century.'[94] If, however, the 'story' had begun, it was by no means complete by the early 1830s, and Linn's case predated both the 1838 Dangerous Lunatics Act, which 'permitted the transfer of an individual from a prison to an asylum if they were considered to be dangerous and either mentally ill or intellectually disabled', and the influential M'Naghten judgment of 1843, which codified the grounds on which an insanity defence could be developed in court.[95] Given this, the question arises as to why the *Northern Whig* and the *Belfast News-Letter* should have reached so quickly for insanity as a means of accounting for John Linn's actions on 29 August 1832.

One obvious answer to this question is that in killing his father Linn had committed an act considered so dreadful that it could only be explained by recourse to insanity. This is superficially plausible, but a degree of caution is nevertheless required. In a study of parricide in early modern England, Walker has demonstrated that while it 'might [be] suppose[d] that insanity would be commonly employed to explain an allegedly unimaginable crime such as parricide' this was not necessarily the case, and 'only a few early modern parricides were explained – and even fewer excused by the courts – as acts of insanity'.[96] Another possibility, however, is that the *Belfast News-Letter* and the *Northern Whig* viewed the murder of William Linn in light of an earlier episode, which had unfolded in Cork in 1828. This was the case of Captain William Stewart and the *Mary Russell*. Crossing the Atlantic from Barbados to Cork in the summer of 1828, Stewart had become convinced that he faced a mutiny and killed seven of his crew. Brought to trial at the Cork assizes of August 1828, he was acquitted on the grounds that he was 'labouring under mental derangement when he committed the act' and placed for two years in Cork gaol, before being moved, in 1830, to a lunatic asylum.[97] This case had at least a tangential connection to Belfast in that the *Mary Russell* had been encountered off the coast of Ireland and brought into Cork by a Belfast vessel named the *Mary Stubbs*.[98] More importantly, however, the case was a well-publicized and widely reported *cause célèbre*.[99] Thus on 1 July 1828, the *Belfast News-Letter* published a short account of the 'shocking occurrence', drawn from a Cork newspaper, and three days later it printed a lengthy report of the initial inquest, which pre-empted the trial in finding that Stewart had been suffering from 'a state of mental derangement'.[100] When the trial itself took place, it received less attention from the *News-Letter*, though the paper did note the verdict, informing readers, on 15 August 1828, that Stewart had been 'acquitted … on the score of his having been insane when he committed the act'.[101]

Whatever influence the *Mary Russell* case might have had on the editorializing of the *Northern Whig* and the *Belfast News-Letter* in August 1832, it must surely have crossed the mind of Chief Justice Bushe as he listened to the evidence concerning John Linn's sanity that was presented the following March. But what of that evidence? First in the witness box was the journeyman Arthur Murphy, who had spent time with Linn in Liverpool and been employed in William Linn's workshop. Under cross-examination, Murphy not only described the agitated state Linn was in when he entered the workshop on the afternoon of 29 August 1832, but detailed a history of troubling behaviour and depicted Linn as a man 'in a distracted state'. He testified that he 'had seen him [Linn] the evening before [William Linn's murder], and he looked not to be in his senses', that some days prior to the murder he had overheard Linn 'shouting, and saying, "he was going mad"' and that, several months previously, he had witnessed a particularly troubling scene in Liverpool, when Linn 'was singing, and at once turned round and said he would go out, and kill some man'. In response to a question from the jury, Murphy also stated that Linn was 'sober' on the day of his father's murder.[102] Quite what the result would have been had he been intoxicated – whether it would have been perceived as an aggravating or a mitigating factor – is unclear. Drunkenness and violent crime often went hand in hand in 19th-century Ireland, but the consequences of killing while under the influence of alcohol could vary: while Vaughan, discussing the commutation of death penalties, has noted that '[a]lcohol … which might suggest absence of deliberation, seemed to make things worse for the prisoner', Pauline Prior has demonstrated that men who killed women could be successfully defended 'on the grounds of temporary insanity due to alcohol consumption'.[103] Whatever the case, Murphy was firm about Linn's sobriety on the day in question. Linn might have been a man of 'dissipated habits', but on 29 August 1829 his 'state of excitement did not arise from drink'.[104]

Murphy's testimony was echoed by that of the two witnesses who were next to the stand: John Heyland and William Walker. Heyland, the blacksmith who had been brought to deal with the locked door of William Linn's house on the day of the murder, explained that Linn 'did not appear drunk, but in a very disturbed state'.[105] Walker, on the other hand, conceded that he was unable so say 'whether [the] prisoner was drunk' on the day in question, but explained that he 'had, sundry times before, seen him very much disturbed, without being in liquor' and that 'his character is that of being frequently in a disturbed state'.[106] Next to give evidence was the police officer, John Dickson, who had been involved in Linn's capture, and the surgeon, John Wales, who had examined William Linn's body, and during whose testimony a 'bloody chisel was produced', adding a frisson of gory excitement to proceedings.[107] Neither man appears to have touched upon Linn's mental state, but decisive evidence on this score was presented by the final witness, Rachel Catherine Peel, née Linn – Linn's sister. Called as a witness for the defence, Peel spoke at length, portraying her brother as a deeply troubled individual. She explained that she had 'for some time past … observed that he [Linn] had a derangement of mind' and that she 'had been from home, for some time, but on her return, observed a great change in his [Linn's] conduct and conversation, particularly toward her father'. Some three years previously, she noted, Linn had suffered a head injury (what this relates to is unclear), and his behaviour had been strange: he had accused their father of 'purchasing poison' and alleged that Peel herself had been planning to kill his sons, an allegation rendered all the more strange by the fact that he had no sons. On top of all this, there were the events, previously mentioned, that she had witnessed on the weekend prior to her father's killing. As the *Northern Whig* reported:

> witness saw prisoner come into the house, went backwards, and examined all the corners: prisoner then went up stairs into the workshop, and, putting up his hands to his head, said, 'Lord Jesus, I am going mad'; witness bound up his head with a handkerchief: soon after which, he took up some of the tools, and said he would murder them all: witness then ran off to get the Police, and fainted.

Having given her account of this troubling episode, Peel was then cross-examined. Once again, the question of Linn's drunkenness came up. Like Murphy and Heyland, Peel denied that Linn had been drunk, before going on to give posthumous voice to her father, explaining that he had told her 'that he was afraid there was something dreadful in his son's hand, as his conduct, of late, was quite changed towards him'. At this point, Chief Justice Bushe intervened: having heard enough, he informed the jury that 'there was abundant proof of the prisoner's insanity' and that it 'ought, at once, to return a verdict to that effect'.[108]

Intriguingly, Bushe later outlined his approach to summing up and charging juries in evidence presented to a select committee enquiring into the state of Ireland. 'I never charge in such a way as to intimate my opinion in facts of the case', he claimed. 'I always explain the law ... but I never intimate the inclination of my mind as to the conclusion to be drawn from controverted facts.'[109] Given this, his actions during Linn's trial appear to have been unusual. However, when he guided the jury on 16 March 1833 Bushe was not formally summing up. Rather, he 'interrupted the examination' of Peel, effectively cutting short the trial. What the jury or the counsels made of this is not recorded, but the former did his bidding, perhaps with a degree of relief, the responsibility for a man's life having effectively been lifted from them. Thus it was that Linn was found 'Not Guilty, he being insane at the time of committing the offence'.[110]

* * *

What, in the final, analysis are we to make of the verdict? Was Linn insane, or did Chief Justice Bushe misdirect his jury? In the absence of a detailed psychological assessment, the latter question is one that cannot be answered conclusively. Nor is it a question that necessarily requires an answer: as Edward Muir and Guido Ruggiero have remarked, 'the value of criminal records for history is not so much what they uncover about a particular crime as what they reveal about otherwise invisible or opaque realms of human experience.'[111] Yet there are a few points that can be made, in closing, concerning the verdict arrived at in March 1833. That Bushe was a judge of many years' experience might, on the surface, encourage a degree of confidence in his assessment. But even experienced judges make mistakes, and it is worth noting that Bushe arrived at the conclusion that Linn had been insane when he killed his father during a busy assizes, and that he appears to have done so only on the basis of anecdotal evidence, without seeking expert testimony regarding Linn's mental state.[112] By contrast, when Linn did come under the observation of those with relevant expertise questions were quickly raised as to whether he was, in fact, insane. It is into the institution in which those question were raised – the Belfast Lunatic Asylum – that we will follow Linn in chapter three.

3. 'So mischievous and unmanageable a character'

On 16 March 1833, at the Co. Antrim assizes, John Linn's story had arrived at a decisive junction. In one direction lay the gallows; in the other, lay the carceral spaces of 19th-century Ulster. As we have seen, Linn's jury was persuaded that he had been 'insane at the time of committing the offence', and found him not guilty. In so doing, they set his story on the latter path.[1]

Accepting that Linn had not been in his right mind on 29 August 1832, led inevitably to the verdict of not guilty. As W.E. Vaughan has remarked: '[i]nsanity, by definition, meant that the prisoner could not be guilty'.[2] But it did not imply that Linn should be released. If not guilty in the sense that he could not be held *responsible* for killing his father, Linn had, nevertheless, killed. He posed an obvious danger, both to the public and himself, and a decision had therefore to be made as to how he was to be dealt with. The responsibility for making this decision lay not in the hands of the judge, Chief Justice Bushe, but in those of the 'royal surrogate', the lord lieutenant of Ireland.[3] As Linn's trial drew to a close, Bushe undertook to 'apprise the Lord Lieutenant of the circumstances', predicting that 'such precautions ... would be taken, in regard to the prisoner, as would prevent him, for the future, from committing any other such savage acts'.[4] Consequently, Linn was 'detained in custody' until, in due course, the then lord lieutenant, Henry William Paget, the first marquess of Anglesey, came to the decision that he should be placed in the Belfast Lunatic Asylum.[5]

* * *

The asylum has been a much discussed institution. In part, this reflects the influence of Michel Foucault, whose 'account of the rise of psychiatry ... is', as Catherine L. Evans has remarked, 'built around the asylum and its analogue, the prison.'[6] Foucault's work has, of course, been subject to critique.[7] Nevertheless, the asylum has continued to attract considerable attention, with recent work moving beyond Foucaultian preoccupations with power and discipline to consider what Catherine Cox has termed 'the consumers of the asylum'.[8] In his own way, Linn, an inmate, may be viewed as a 'consumer' of the Belfast Lunatic Asylum. But before turning to consider his experience of the institution, we may first consider its establishment, and its significance as a site of administrative dispute.

Thanks to the early date at which its network of state-mandated asylums was established, Ireland occupies a distinctive place in the wider history of the asylum. 'What England saw only in 1845, or France in 1838,' Mark Finnane has noted, 'Ireland had already witnessed in its essentials in 1817: the legislative provision of public asylums for the entire country.'[9] Well-rehearsed in the relevant literature, the early history of Ireland's asylum system need not detain us here. It is sufficient to note that in the late 18th and early 19th centuries Irish asylum provision was limited; that reformers, including Sir John Newport, MP for Waterford, and Thomas Spring Rice, MP for Limerick, campaigned for its enlargement; and that Robert Peel, in his capacity as chief secretary for Ireland, took an interest in the matter, initiating inquiries that led in July 1817 to the introduction of a bill (57 Geo. III, c. 106) to facilitate the establishment of a series of 'district asylums' that would augment existing institutions in Dublin and Cork. This was amended, a number of times in the years that followed, and by the mid-1830s nine new asylums had been opened – asylums that were controlled ultimately by the lord lieutenant and that included the institution into which John Linn was placed in 1833, the Belfast 'District Hospital, for the treatment of the Insane' (henceforth, the Belfast Lunatic Asylum).[10]

Located 'in the immediate vicinity of the town, a little to the west', on a site occupied today by the Royal Victoria Hospital, the Belfast Lunatic Asylum was an impressive building, set in airy grounds. Writing in the late 1830s, P.D. Hardy remarked that it 'arrests the eye for several miles before entering Belfast', and noted that it was 'a well-constructed edifice, admirably fitted for the purposes to which it is devoted'. Work on the building had begun in 1827, and it opened, two years later, in 1829.[11] Viewed one way, the institution appears as a local manifestation of a government policy that had been inaugurated with the legislative provision of 1817. But it would be inaccurate to suggest that the asylum was foisted on Belfast by government. In his mid-19th century *History of the General Hospital, Belfast, and the other medical institutions of the town*, the Belfast physician A.G. Malcolm observed that in November 1825 committee members of the Belfast Medical Society joined with committee members from the Belfast Charitable Society and the House of Industry 'to induce the government … to fix on Belfast as the most proper site for the new Lunatic Asylum.' Malcolm went on to concede that it was unclear if these efforts 'had any influence in directing the site of the Belfast Asylum', but it is nevertheless significant that they were made.[12] Existing scholarship has sought an explanation for the precipitate development of Ireland's 19th-century asylum system in the colonial nature of government in Ireland, from 1801 a part of the United Kingdom, but one in which 'metropolitan trappings' rubbed alongside a 'colonial political architecture', represented, most obviously, by the lord lieutenant and the Dublin administration.[13] However, if it is true, as Finnane has argued, that the establishment of Ireland's asylum system 'was facilitated by the "colonial colour" of … government', the fact that some within the medical and philanthropic circles of early 19th-century Belfast lobbied for the construction of an asylum in their town indicates that the Belfast Lunatic Asylum was rather more than a colonial imposition.[14] It was an institution that some, at least, were invested in, and this sense of investment was made manifest in two disputes that are known to have taken place between the lord lieutenant and the asylum's board of governors.

The best-known of these disputes occurred during the 1840s and 50s, when, as Pauline Prior and David Griffith have detailed, the asylum's board of governors defied the lord lieutenant by refusing to appoint a chaplain. This dispute ended in the Court of Queen's Bench in Dublin in January 1856, where the governors triumphed, and it was judged that the lord lieutenant did not have the right to compel them to appoint, and pay, a chaplain. Prior and Griffith have viewed the episode as indicative of a 'deep-seated resentment of colonial administration', suggesting that it was 'the public face of an ongoing power struggle between local landed interests and colonial rulers'.[15] This is, perhaps, to overstate the case: whether or not the asylum's board of governors considered themselves to be subject to 'colonial rulers' is moot. It is, however, clear that there was some precedent to the dispute. Prior and Griffiths note that the board of governors had, in 1847, opposed plans to expand Ulster's existing asylums and open a new facility in Omagh, and the asylum's proceedings book reveals details of an earlier dispute between the board of governors and the lord lieutenant – a dispute concerning the presence of John Linn within the institution.[16]

Linn first entered the Belfast Lunatic Asylum on 28 March 1833, and within a matter of weeks questions were raised as to whether or not it was appropriate for him to remain there.[17] At a meeting of the asylum's board of governors, held on 6 May 1833, it was 'Resolved that the certificate of Doctor McDonnell [the asylum's 'Visiting Physician'] and statement respecting the condition of Linn by the Manager [Mr Cuming] be transmitted to Sir Wm Gosset [under-secretary in the Dublin administration] representing that the man is no longer a subject for the Asylum and requesting that he may be removed.'[18] The grounds on which Linn was judged unsuitable for confinement within the asylum were not made clear in the record of the meeting, but a later entry in the proceedings book is more explicit: Linn was considered to be 'in a state of perfect sanity'.[19] Concerns regarding Linn's presence in the asylum were discussed by the board of governors for a second time on 3 June 1833. The manager of the asylum, a Mr Cuming, 'represented his apprehension that the convict John Linn, respecting whom a representation was directed to be made to Sir Gosset, might endeavour to make his escape', and it was agreed that he should 'communicate the same to Sir Gosset in order to expedite the removal of this man'.[20] This seemed to do the trick, for when the board of governors met next, on 1 July 1833, a communication from Gosset was read, and it was determined: 'That in pursuance of the direction contained therein, the Manager be requested to have John Linn removed from this Asylum to the County Antrim Gaol as soon as possible'.[21] Thus far, the story seems unremarkable. Placed in the asylum late in March 1833, Linn was quickly discovered to be sane, and a successful representation was made to the lord lieutenant, via William Gosset, following which he was moved to a more suitable place of confinement. But some thirteen months later, in August 1834, the story took another turn, when Linn was returned to the asylum 'by order of the Lord Lieutenant'.[22]

The reason for the lord lieutenant's order is unclear, though it is possible that Linn was returned to the asylum in response to overcrowding within the Co. Antrim gaol, located in Carrickfergus, for the 'defective state' of the gaol's 'accommodation' was, by 1834, well-known.[23] Whatever the case, it is clear that the asylum's board of governors was far from happy with this turn of events. Thus, on 1 September 1834 Cuming was instructed to provide Gosset with copies of previous correspondence and paperwork relating to Linn, and to 'state that he and the Physician are still of opinion that Linn is not a fit subject for this Asylum, and the Governors consider him such a dangerous person that they desire immediate removal, for the welfare of the establishment'.[24] This Cuming did, but at the next meeting of the board of governors, held early in October 1834, he reported that he had 'received no answer to his communication'. Consequently, he was directed to write again to Gosset, 'begging his early attention to the former communication' and stressing that Linn was 'not a fit object' for the asylum and that he was 'occupying room which is greatly needed for the accommodation of persons, for whose use the Asylum was instituted'.[25] By this point, space was at a premium within the asylum. In 1833, it had been reported that its inmates 'far exceeded what it was originally intended to contain' and by 1834 alterations were made to its 'interior arrangements', 'by which accommodation has been provided for 50 patients above the number for which the house was originally designed.'[26] Notwithstanding this, the board of governors' concerns fell on deaf ears, for by November 1834 they had received a communication from Gosset's superior, the chief secretary, Edward John Littleton, indicating that the lord lieutenant had resolved 'that Linn must remain in the asylum'.[27] In response to this, the board sought outside assistance, agreeing that the chief secretary's communication should be made known 'to the Bishop of Down who is at present in Dublin', and that he should be asked to 'take such steps to obtain a reversion of the decision as he may deem expedient'.[28] The bishop obliged the board, but to no avail: 'Sir Wm Gosset … repeated to him the decision of the Lord Lieutenant, that John Linn, should remain in the Asylum', explaining 'that the Lord Lieutenant judged it right for the man to be detained in custody, and that the Lord Chief Justice of the Kings Bench, was of opinion, that the Asylum was the proper place for detaining him'.[29]

At this point, it appears as though the Dublin establishment had closed ranks in the face of the board of governors' continued entreaties. The board itself was initially minded to persist, resolving, in December 1834, that 'another communication be made to the Government', but whether this communication was made, or a response received, is not recorded, and for several months thereafter Linn's presence in the asylum appears to have been accepted.[30] In October 1835, however, an opportunity arose to resurrect the issue. Several months previously, in April 1835, Constantine Henry Phipps, the second earl of Mulgrave, was appointed as lord lieutenant.[31] Mulgrave was, as Peter Gray has remarked, 'the most popular lord lieutenant in the institution's history', and an important means whereby he cultivated and maintained his popularity were his 'provincial tours', which provided 'the opportunity of engaging in the politics of spectacle'.[32] Late in October 1835 Belfast provided a stage for one such display, when Mulgrave visited the town and toured a number of its better-known institutions, including the Lancastrian School, the Royal Belfast Academical Institution, the Belfast Academy, the House of Correction and the Belfast Lunatic Asylum.[33]

On the surface, Mulgrave's visit to the asylum passed off without incident. He was 'received with all due honours at the grand entrance gate, by the Board of Governors' and after closely inspecting the institution he instructed his attendant, Colonel Yorke, to 'make a memorandum of the complete satisfaction he felt at thus, by careful personal observation, being enabled highly to approve of its moral management, and most creditable appearance in every respect'.[34] Behind the scenes, however, there was more going on than the polite posturing of civic ceremony. The asylum's board of governors seized the opportunity presented by Mulgrave's visit and 'directed his ... attention to the case of John Linn'. The lord lieutenant was advised that 'several applications had been made ... at different times to have him removed', and that he was considered 'in the opinion of both the Physician and Manager an unfit subject for such an Institution'. Were all of this not enough, it was reinforced by a petition from Linn himself, who requested that the lord lieutenant 'would order his removal to one of His Majesty's foreign colonies.' Placed in an awkward position, Mulgrave stalled. He 'expressed his desire to meet the wishes of the Governors', but added an important qualification: 'he was of opinion that John Linn having taken a fellow creature's life, was not a proper person to be at large in a foreign land any more than in his own country'. Notwithstanding this, he undertook 'to take the case into his consideration on his return to Dublin', and early in December his response to Linn's 'petiton' was received.[35] From the board's perspective, it was a disappointing one: Mulgrave held firm, refusing to 'sanction the discharge of any person who having taken the life of another saved his own only on the plea of insanity'. But by this point the question was purely academic, for just a few weeks previously, on the night of the 20–1 November, Linn had taken matters into his own hands, escaping 'through the window of the cell in which he was confined'.[36]

Three points emerge from this protracted administrative wrangle. First, it is clear that Linn did not remain in the Belfast Lunatic Asylum throughout the period from late March 1833, when he was first placed in the institution, to November 1835, when he escaped. As we have seen, he was moved to

Carrickfergus gaol in July 1833, and remained there until August 1834, when he was returned to the asylum. Secondly, it is clear that the way in which Linn should be viewed was quickly called into question. Within the asylum, Linn was judged sane, and by December 1835 even the lord lieutenant appears to have conceded that Linn 'having taken the life of another [had] saved his own only on the plea of insanity'. From an early point, therefore, Linn's experience of confinement and imprisonment was characterized by instability – both spatial, as he moved from asylum to prison and back again, and conceptual, as he was classified initially as someone of unsound mind, before being reassessed and identified as someone who was sane, and therefore unsuitable for confinement within the asylum. Finally, the asylum's negotiation with the lord lieutenant indicates that the tensions of the 1840s and 50s were not *sui generis*, and that Belfast's asylum, an institution managed by a local board of governors, but ultimately controlled by the lord lieutenant, had emerged as a site of administrative conflict, in which the judgment of the lord lieutenant was questioned and contested at a much earlier date.

* * *

From one perspective, then, the Belfast Lunatic Asylum appears as a site of administrative dispute in which conflict and negotiation took place between the state, represented by the lord lieutenant, and civil society, represented by the board of governors.[37] This dynamic was by no means unique to Belfast. Working on the asylum system in the southeast of Ireland, Cox has recently explored the ways in which 'civil society negotiated the institutionalization of the mentally ill', foregrounding 'the extent to which, in local contexts, protagonists … resisted and manoeuvred around the boundaries of the formal, centralized asylum and workhouse systems'.[38] Such interactions offer valuable local perspectives on the much discussed development of government in nineteenth-century Ireland, taking us beyond the idea of a 'centralizing interventionist state' and bearing out Virginia Crossman's recent observation that 'the growth of the state in the nineteenth century was a more complex process than is often suggested'.[39]

But if it was a space of administrative dispute, the Belfast Lunatic Asylum was also a space of science, in which the insane were treated humanely and enlightened theories prevailed.[40] In general terms, as David N. Livingstone has argued, attitudes towards the asylum shifted during the 19th century, and it came to be viewed by some 'as a progressive institution'. This development was made manifest in architecture and landscaping. 'Inside,' Livingstone writes, 'asylums were to be spacious, airy, and elegant, fitted out with galleries, and music rooms; outside, they were to be positioned on elevated sites and surrounded by gracious gardens with extensive walks.'[41] Set beyond the town's western boundary, and boasting a 'spacious area in front, which serves as a garden and exercise space for patients', Belfast's asylum reflected this 'progressive' shift.[42] Indeed, while the asylum building was panoptical, suggesting surveillance and constraint, the way in which its residents were treated was more humane than its architectural form might at first imply.[43] As R.J. McClelland has detailed, the asylum system that developed in Ireland from the late 1810s was one that 'incorporated the "moral" approach to treatment from its outset, characterised by humanness and work therapy', and Belfast's asylum was overseen, from 1835 onwards, in a particularly enlightened manner.[44] In April 1835, the then manager of the asylum, Mr Cuming, moved to Swift's Hospital in Dublin, and in due course Dr Robert Stuart was appointed as his replacement.[45] A former student of Glasgow University, Stuart's approach to the care of the insane was shaped by that of Glasgow's professor of medicine and chemistry, Robert Cleghorn. In addition to his professorial role, Cleghorn served as the Glasgow asylum's physician 'and had a clear policy of minimizing restraint'; Stuart adopted a similar approach in Belfast, and under his guidance the town's lunatic asylum 'attained a high reputation for the skill and humanity which guided its administration.'[46]

Alongside the application of cutting-edge approaches to treatment, attempts were also made to develop new forms of knowledge within the Belfast Lunatic Asylum, and here Linn played a role. As has already been noted, one of the most useful sources we have concerning Linn's story is an article published in the *Phrenological Journal* in 1836. Attributed to R.C. – most likely Robert Cox, one of the *Phrenological Journal*'s editors – this article contains transcriptions of letters written by John Grattan, a businessman with interests in phrenology who had visited Linn in the asylum.[47] That Linn should have received attention from those engaging with phrenology – 'a combined theory of brain and a science of character', which proposed, among other things, that 'the brain is not a homogenous unity but an aggregate of mental organs' and that 'external craniological means can be used to diagnose the internal state of the mental faculties' – is by no means surprising.[48] Phrenology was, as Roger Cooter has remarked, 'the nineteenth century's most popular and popularized "science"', and its advocates often sought to apply their 'insights' to the 'criminal mind'.[49] In Belfast, a distinct phrenological 'moment' can be identified in the late 1820s and early 1830s. A short-lived phrenological society was established in the town in 1827, and three years later, in 1830, the well-known phrenologist Johann Gaspar Spurzheim delivered a series of lectures in the Belfast Academical Institution.[50] These prompted heated debate in the columns of Belfast's newspapers, but it is nevertheless clear that some within the town's medical and scientific circles viewed phrenology as a credible form of knowledge.[51]

This group included James Lawson Drummond, professor of anatomy and botany at the Royal Belfast Academical Institution, who provided a testimonial for the prominent Scottish phrenologist George Coombe when he applied for the chair of logic at Edinburgh University in 1836, and it likely also included Dr

James M'Donnell, 'the Nestor of science in Belfast'.[52] M'Donnell served as the lunatic asylum's 'Visiting Physician' until 1837, and it was thanks to him that the attentions of the wider phrenological community were directed towards Linn.[53] As R.C. explained in the *Phrenological Journal*, M'Donnell had sent 'a cast of the head of John Linn of Belfast, who had been found guilty of parricide … to the Phrenological Society [most likely of Edinburgh]' and it was as a result of this that 'we were induced to make inquiry into the history and character of the criminal'.[54] This 'inquiry' was pursued remotely, making use of John Grattan, whose research was facilitated by M'Donnell: as Grattan himself noted, 'Dr M'Donnell, who is the medical attendant of the lunatic asylum … most kindly gave me such information as he possessed concerning him [i.e., Linn], and also a ticket of admission for Mr Wales and myself to see him.'[55]

Within the asylum, then, Linn became a subject of scientific investigation as phrenologists sought to make sense of his case and, indeed, his character: having viewed the cast of Linn's head, and considered the information supplied by Grattan, R.C. concluded that Linn's 'largest organs' were 'Combativeness, Destructiveness, Secretiveness, Cautiousness, Amativeness, and Acquisitiveness', and that his 'dispositions were quarrelsome and violent'.[56] Quite what Linn himself made of all this is unclear. The procedure whereby a cast of his head was made he no doubt experienced as disagreeable, involving, as it did, the placement of breathing tubes in the nostrils and the covering of the face with layers of plaster.[57] There is some evidence, too, to suggest that he found his notoriety to be a source of frustration. Thus, in his account of visiting the asylum, Grattan noted that Linn 'at first appeared to dislike being recognized' and resisted attempts to discuss what he had come to describe as the 'unfortunate occurrence' – that is, his killing of his father.[58] At the same time, however, the attention Linn received presented something of an opportunity. When Grattan visited Linn in the asylum with John Wales – 'the surgeon who attended the inquest [of William Linn], and who knew Linn well' – Linn explained that 'he always loved his father, and would have done anything for him; but that his sister had turned him, the father, against him'.[59] He sought 'to convince Mr. Wales that he was not insane, and had been perfectly free from any thing even like temporary insanity since his admission into the asylum', explaining that there was 'nothing to excite him' and that he had no access to 'spirituous drink', which had had an 'uncontrollable influence upon him'; and, despite his reluctance to discuss his killing of his father, he made a particular effort to correct an inaccurate story concerning that event.[60] As Grattan related:

> He was extraordinarily solicitous to contradict an erroneous report which he stated had been circulated concerning him, and which charged him with having *torn and destroyed the Bible* before that 'unfortunate occurrence.' He repeated this several times, evidently regarding it as a more heinous offence than the crime of which he was actually guilty.[61]

Linn's awareness of this 'erroneous report' suggests that inmates of the asylum were not cut off entirely from wider society, and that gossip and rumour penetrated the institution's walls. But more significant are the glimpses Grattan's account offers of Linn attempting to manage his reputation and make sense of his situation. Categorized by the legal system as insane, and treated accordingly by the lord lieutenant, Linn used the opportunity of Grattan's visit to assert his sanity, offer his perspective on his relationship with his father and correct the record concerning what had actually taken place on 29 August 1832. In short, the attention he received from phrenologists provided Linn with an opportunity to quietly exercise agency and tell his story, or at least a part of it, in his own terms.

Further examples of Linn's attempts to exercise agency within the asylum can be found in its proceedings book. In September 1835, for example, the board of governors took into consideration '[a]n application ... by letter from John Linn requesting that he may be employed to whitewash and plaister [*sic*] the Asylum'. This they rejected, resolving 'that John Linn be informed that no inmate of the Institution is entitled to or can be paid by the Board any compensation for work which he may do the same being required from every inmate capable of working as a return for their support'.[62] The proceedings book also makes reference to two appeals Linn made to the lord lieutenant: a 'Memorial', requesting 'discharge from the Asylum', which received a negative response in February 1835; and the later petition, which was passed to the earl of Mulgrave when he visited the asylum in October 1835.[63] The second of these documents, which survives in a convict reference file, makes for interesting reading. As was the case when he met with Grattan and Wales, Linn sought to establish his sanity, though his insistence that he had 'not shewed the least symptom of Insanity since it pleased God to restore him to his reason, which is now about three years ago', contains a tacit acknowledgment that he had, for a time, been mentally incapacitated. He asserted that he was 'a strong healthy young man, and a good tradesman, both able, and willing to support his wife and children by honest industry', and alluded, knowledgably to scripture. Noting that the lord lieutenant had granted 'royal clemency to a good number of individuals, some of whose offences may be like the Debtor mentioned by our Saviour in the Holy Scriptures, who owed only fifty pence', he conceded that his own offence 'may have amounted to the full sum of five hundred pence like the other Debtor', but pointed out that both debtors were 'frankly forgiven'.[64] In seeking release, Linn thus represented himself as a hardworking man who knew his Scripture, had recovered his sanity and wanted only to support his family. As we have seen, Mulgrave was not convinced. But by the time his opinion was known Linn had exercised his agency in an altogether more overt way, by absconding from the asylum.[65]

* * *

As might be expected, Linn returned to the columns of Belfast's newspapers in the days following his flight from the asylum. His escape was reported in the *Guardian and Constitutional Advocate*, the *Belfast News-Letter* and the *Northern Whig*, with the latter going into some detail.[66] It appears that Linn had been 'regularly locked up' on the evening of Friday, 20 November 1835, and that he was discovered, the following morning, to have 'disappeared': he had made his way through the window of his cell, an operation which required him to detach 'with the aid of some blunt instrument, the lowermost portion of the window frame', and had succeeded, 'with the assistance of a plank', in climbing the asylum's 'boundary wall'. Noting that it was 'supposed probable, that he will endeavour making off to America', the *Whig* suggested that this was, on balance, a good thing, reasoning that:

> it will be a happy riddance to this part of the country, in which, long previously to the atrocious and unnatural crime he had imbrued his hands in, he was a dread and a terror, by reason of an innate lawlessness and ferociousness of disposition, which was termed insanity, – but, in point of fact, was nothing more or less than the working of a most ungovernable and turbulent temper, excited into action by too free a use of ardent spirits.

To this, it added the observations that Linn's 'appearance was … forbidding and repulsive in the extreme, being well calculated to alarm even more than the timorous'; that his residence in the asylum was 'frequently represented to Government as being by no means a fitting place for such a criminal character'; and that 'even in the County Jail it was found difficult enough to keep in subjection, so reckless a spirit as the parricidal and other shocking actions he was guilty of proved him to be'.[67] Here, as in the proceedings book of the lunatic asylum, we see Linn being presented not as insane, but as criminal – and here, too, we see something of his notoriety among contemporaries. Where the phrenologists sought to understand and make some sense of Linn's case – albeit according to the dictates of their 'science' – the *Northern Whig* presented him in an almost cartoonish fashion as a 'dread and a terror', a man gripped by an 'ungovernable and turbulent temper', whose appearance was 'forbidding and repulsive' and whose crimes were a reflection of his 'reckless … spirit'.

In the aftermath of his escape, Linn disappeared without trace. As the weeks and months passed it no doubt seemed as though he was gone for good, but early in September 1836 he reappeared in what were, by now, typically dramatic circumstances. As the *Freeman's Journal* reported on 3 September, he had been arrested a few days previously on Dublin's Fleet Street following a 'desperate resistance', and had 'confessed that he lately shot a man in Liverpool, and threatened soon to go to Belfast where his wife resided, for the purpose of killing her, after which he said he intended to commit suicide'.[68] Two days later, Belfast's *Northern Whig* reported the arrest, offering further details and, as in November 1835, when it had reported on his escape from the lunatic asylum, a pointed comment on his character:

> Alderman Durley, on getting information of his being in Dublin, placed a warrant for his apprehension in the hands of two officers, Messrs. Roberts and Hartley. They found him in an eating-house, in Fleet-street, reading a newspaper. One of them sat down beside him, and the other opposite to him. After some conversation, in the course of which he called himself M'Gouran, they were satisfied that he was the person described; and, one of them caught his arms, while the other sprang forward in front. He struggled hard, and attempted to take out two loaded detonating pistols from the breast of his coat. It appears, from his own confession, that he had taken his passage at Liverpool, for America; that the vessel was obliged to return; that he went on shore, where the Police of the port attempted to arrest him; and that, having shot one of them, he fled to Dublin. He has been sent to Kilmainham Jail. The Police had to get a float to convey him, as no force could have got him into a coach. He says he intended coming to Belfast, to murder his wife and children, and then shoot himself. Linn, on his conviction for the murder of his father, was treated as a lunatic; but the fact is, that he is no farther a lunatic than his savage and brutal disposition and temper make him; and he should, unquestionably, be put in some other place of safe keeping than a Lunatic Asylum.[69]

That Linn should have violently resisted arrest is entirely plausible, but there are grounds on which to question the more sensational aspects of these reports. Take, for example, Linn's alleged claim to have shot a man in Liverpool. Attempts were made to investigate this – a report in *The Standard*, a London newspaper, noted that '[a] letter has been sent to Liverpool to inquire into the transaction which he declares he was concerned in there' – but there is no further reference to legal action being taken, casting doubt on Linn's 'confession'.[70] And what of his supposedly murderous and suicidal intentions? Here, too, a degree of circumspection is advisable. An individual as notorious as Linn plainly was invariably became the subject of spurious and lurid rumour. In Belfast, as we have already seen, it was claimed that he had 'torn and destroyed' a Bible prior to killing his father, and shocking reports clearly circulated more widely. When the *Caledonian Mercury* reported on his arrest in 1836, it observed that he had earlier been 'tried for the murder of his father under circumstances of unparalleled atrocity, having cut off his head with a hatchet.'[71] Given all of this, it is entirely possible that the claims that Linn had planned to travel to Belfast and murder his family, before killing himself, were exaggerated, or even invented. But what is significant is that they were considered credible: such, by September 1836, was the extent of Linn's notoriety.

If the more dramatic details that circulated at the time of Linn's arrest are open to question, what of the claim that he had attempted to sail for America from Liverpool? Here we are on firmer ground, for Linn himself later gave an account of his movements that aligns with the *Northern Whig*'s report on this point. In his own telling, upon escaping from the lunatic asylum Linn received assistance, in the form of clothes and money, from an unnamed 'acquaintance', and made for Scotland. There he secured employment, and 'saved as much money, by Careful Honest Industry, as would have taken him to New York in America, where he intended to go, had the Vessel in which he was, not run a Sand Bank, & from the injuries she received, been forced to return to Liverpool'. This account is to be found in a second petition that Linn made to the lord lieutenant – a petition in which he complained of his treatment, declaring that it was 'very Extraordinary and Inconsistent, that the same Law, which made him unaccountable for his Actions … should at the same time make him Accountable, by keeping him in a doleful Prison', and requested that he be given 'a free passage to America, or one of her Majesty's Foreign Colonies'. More interesting than the complaint Linn made concerning his own treatment, however, is the fact that he made reference to his children when petitioning the lord lieutenant. Alleged by the *Northern Whig* to have been planning their murder in September 1836, Linn appears in his petition in a very different light, decrying the fact that his 'innocent Offspring' were 'Suffering Extreme Misery in Consequence of his long Confinement'.[72] This was not, moreover, the only occasion on which Linn evinced an awareness of his children's suffering. In his earlier petition, passed to the lord lieutenant at the time of his visit to the Belfast Lunatic Asylum in October 1835, he noted that he 'had a wife, and four small helpless infants, who were involved in the greatest misery and distress, being destitute of all means of support and [-] existing on the gratuitous bounty of others, till two of them died.'[73]

A glimpse of the fate of these unfortunate children can be found in the records of the Belfast Charitable Society. First established as early as 1752, the Charitable Society had, in 1774, opened a Poor House 'for the reception of the aged and infirm, and the support and instruction of destitute children'.[74] By the mid-1830s, this was a well-established Belfast institution, which provided accommodation for significant numbers of needy children. 'Between the years 1821 and 1846', R.W.M. Strain noted, in his standard history of the Charitable Society, 'there were never less than 100 children in the House, and at one time as many as 242.'[75] Their number included three of Linn's children – Anna Isabella, Maria Caroline and Martha Linn – whose entry to the Poor House was recorded on 7 June 1834; that only three were admitted suggests that the fourth Linn child was, by this point, already dead.[76]

The three surviving children entered the Poor House at an unpropitious time. In October 1832, allegations were made that the children in the Poor House 'were badly fed, badly clothed, and badly educated, and that there is scarcely a single pupil in the children's school, or infant's school, who is not over-run with scrofula'. The Charitable Society's committee rebutted these charges, but there were clearly problems within the Poor House, and in May 1835 its schoolmistress, Barbara Ferris, was sacked, following claims that she had treated her charges with 'unnecessary harshness'.[77] When we add to these details the notoriety of their father and the associated familial disgrace – as Jade Shepherd has recently noted, 'shame attached to both criminality and insanity' – then there are ample grounds on which to suspect that the Linn girls' experience of the Poor House was a deeply unhappy one.[78] It was also, for Martha Linn, fleeting. On 13 May 1835, less than a year after entering the Poor House, she passed away. Her entry in the records of Belfast's New Burial Ground confirms that John Linn was her father, and records her age: she was just six years old. Two-and-a-half years later, on 2 November 1837, a third of Linn's children, Maria Caroline, also died. Intriguingly, she is described in the New Burial Ground's records as an 'Orphan'.[79] This was not, of course, the case: John Linn, her father, was alive, but it is possible that he was, by this point, disregarded as a parent as a result of his circumstances, and that his surviving children were looked on as orphans following the death of their mother, though when this occurred is unknown.

Overall, these melancholy details raise more questions than they answer. What became of Linn's wife? Why was it necessary to place the Linn children in the Poor House in 1834? Who had provided for them in the period prior to their entry, and why did they stop doing so? Why was John Linn identified as a father in 1835, but not in November 1837? And what of Linn's sisters and their husbands? Did they take an interest in the fate of their nieces, or were the children disowned following their father's trial? While such questions must remain unanswered, they serve to foreground the fact that Linn's story is not just the story of one man, but of a family. As Shepherd has demonstrated in relation to 19th-century England, confinement in an asylum could have multiple impacts on the families of the confined, 'potentially not only causing poverty but also bringing about the temporary or permanent reconfiguration of the family, developing reliance upon kinship networks to maintain the family's health and integrity, and shaping familial relationships'.[80] For the children of John Linn, there was to be no such reconfiguration, and the consequences of their father's crime and confinement proved devastating. Left without a functioning support network, they were pitched into destitution, and in this sense the story of John Linn may be viewed as a family tragedy.

* * *

But what of John Linn? How did his story unfold in the months following his arrest in Dublin in September 1836? Inevitably, his recapture resurrected the question as to where he should be confined. Well aware of this, the governors of the Belfast Lunatic Asylum met on 5 September 1836, agreeing:

> That a Memorial be forthwith transmitted to the Lord Lieutenant … praying His Excellency to make such an order for the disposal of the said John Linn as may preserve the welfare of an Institution of the greatest value to the community at large and to its unoffending inmates in particular from being endangered by the compulsory admittance into it of so mischievous and unmanageable a character …'[81]

In due course, the lord lieutenant responded, advising that Linn was 'to be detained in confinement in Kilmainham Gaol'.[82] The asylum's board of governors was no doubt relieved, but perhaps also frustrated: much trouble could have been avoided had their earlier warnings been heeded. In public, however, the lord lieutenant's decision was praised. The *Northern Whig* opined that it was 'only what we expected, from His Excellency's well known judgement and discrimination', though it used the opportunity to stress, once again, that Linn was not a lunatic, and to argue for his transportation to a penal colony. Linn, the paper insisted, was 'quite sane, but so completely lost to every moral principle, and so depraved by habit, that to him no crime was too great for his perpetration, when his temper became unbridled'; the best course of action would be 'to send him to some of the condemned establishments, in Australia; and, by having him chained at work, try to make him feel the enormity of his crime, and break down his ferocious temper.'[83]

Linn was to remain in Dublin's Kilmainham gaol for the best part of a year. However, on 3 July 1837 he was discharged and moved, 'by order of Government', to the Co. Antrim gaol, located in Carrickfergus.[84] This was an institution in which Linn was well-known: as we have seen, he spent the period from July 1833 to August 1834 in the gaol, and he had earlier been confined in it for a short spell following an assault on his father in July 1832.[85] It was also an institution that had long been subject to criticism, and that was mired in bureaucratic torpor. On a day-to-day basis, the gaol was well run. Its governor, James Erskine, appears to have been active and efficient, and in 1826 the annual report of the inspectors general of Irish prisons made reference to its 'zealous and good officers'.[86] This praise of the prison's 'officers' was echoed in 1827, when they were said to be 'unusually well qualified for their office and zealous to do their duty', and in 1829, when they were described as 'zealous and active in their various duties', but it was bestowed against a backdrop of sweeping censure.[87] The gaol had been extended in the late 1810s, but by the mid-1820s it was clear that it was unfit for purpose.[88] 'It is much to be regretted', the inspectors general complained, in their 1823 report, 'that a new prison was not erected instead of the additions, which have created great difficulty in classification, and rendered it impracticable as to the extent which the law requires.'[89] This set the tone for future reports. In 1824, for instance, it was noted that the gaol 'does not contain any of the modern improvements as to structure, which constitutes the groundwork for classification, industry and moral reformation', that there were no 'work rooms' and that 'the classification is defective for want of accommodation, the tried and untried criminals associating together', and the 1825 report complained that 'the want of accommodation for classification and labour, and the bad structure of this prison, must ever act as a preventative to great moral improvement and good order'.[90] By 1826, there was a glimmer of hope: the grand jury was considering the possibility of erecting a new gaol for Co. Antrim.[91] The decision-making process was, however, painfully slow. In 1830 it was agreed that a new gaol *was* required, but the question as to where it should be located was unresolved.[92] By the mid-1830s no agreement had been reached, and the Carrickfergus gaol was as crowded and unsatisfactory as ever.[93] 'There are but 50 cells for an average of 120 prisoners,' the inspectors general observed, in their 1836 report, 'and there were confined on the day of inspection, 168 prisoners ... the tried and the untried are together, contrary to law; there are frequently from 40 to 50 men in one small day-room, and three or four in a cell at night.'[94]

Under such circumstances there was an inevitable potential for mischief, and for hardened criminals to corrupt their fellow prisoners: 'on one day', the inspectors general complained, in their 1833 report, 'there were 283 persons confined; the tried and untried, the felon and the minor offender, necessarily mixed together, and contaminating each other'.[95] When he was moved from Kilmainham to Carrickfergus in July 1837, Linn was thus moved to a crowded gaol in which inmates had the opportunity to interact and the strong could influence the weak. An individual such as Linn presented an obvious danger in an environment of this nature, but he appeared outwardly to present few problems. The gaol's governor, James Erskine, later recalled that he had 'behaved remarkably well' and 'was appointed a monitor, and also to ask a blessing at the meals', and there is evidence also to suggest that he played a role in enforcing discipline within the prison: a fellow inmate, Michael Walter Cash, later related that 'Linn had often quelled disturbances in gaol'.[96] But behind this conformist façade Linn remained as troublesome as ever, and early in February 1838 it came to light that he was 'the principal leader and instigator' in 'a Plot or Combination ... formed under oath by a number of prisoners for the purpose of violently attempting to make their escape on the first favourable opportunity'.[97]

In an earlier account of this plot, Keith Haines has surmised that 'attempted escapes ... were relatively common'.[98] There is much evidence to bear this out. In September 1816, the brothers John and Robert Greer, whose trial for parricide was discussed in chapter two, attempted to escape from Carrickfergus gaol by 'cutting the iron bars' in a cell window. As a result, they were 'heavily ironed', but this did not prevent the older of the two brothers, John Greer, from making a second, more audacious escape attempt towards the end of December 1816.[99] As the *Belfast News-Letter* reported, he placed, in his bed, 'a figure made up to resemble him with a night cap on' and when this was discovered and the alarm raised he was found hiding in a wooden sentry post, 'fully equipped for his journey, having on his person a horn filled with gunpowder, two knives and a large gimlet, and beside him was found a rope ladder very ingeniously constructed, and a small grapling [*sic*] iron to attach it to'.[100] Three years later, when renovation work was being carried out to extend the gaol, a group of twelve men attempted to escape; nine were caught in the act, but three succeeded.[101] At around the same time, escapes and attempted escapes occurred in gaols in Armagh, Carlow, Drogheda, Londonderry ('by 10 Offenders, some of them charged with Murder and Burglaries') and Maryborough ('of Eight desperate Villains'), and further examples can be found in the reports returned by the inspectors general of Ireland's prisons during the 1820s and 1830s.[102] In 1826, for example, it was reported that there had, in the previous year, been 'repeated attempts at escape' from the Co. Longford gaol, and reference was made to escapes from the Thomastown Bridewell.[103] Likewise, the 1830 report made reference to escapes and attempted escapes from gaols and bridewells in Cavan, Westmeath, Caherciveen, Dungarvan and Wicklow, and the 1836 report noted that 'the Governor (with other officers)' of the Co. Waterford gaol was 'removed', following an 'inquiry which recently took place on the occasion of the escape of convicts and other prisoners of this gaol'.[104]

Viewed in this light, the fact that an escape plot was uncovered in Carrickfergus in 1838 was not, in itself, remarkable: escapes and escape attempts were a recurrent feature of the Irish carceral system. Two things, however, mark the 1838 plot out as noteworthy: the involvement of Linn, and its scale. The plot had first come to light on 5 February 1838 when the governor of the prison, James Erskine, was advised by an inmate 'named John McClean who acts as one of the Cooks' – whether or not this was the John M'Lean that Linn had clashed with in Belfast in 1825 is unknown – that 'there was a very serious Plan going on amongst the Prisoners in the Crown Yard ... to effect their escape', and that the plan was 'headed' by Linn. A day later, on 6 February, Erskine received further information. A second prisoner, John Crossan, requested a private meeting and confirmed both that there was a plot, and that Linn, who was 'armed with a strong sharp instrument', was one of its leaders. Thus informed, Erskine decided to act. Linn was summoned and, 'after a desperate struggle', in which Erskine was 'assisted by 5 men', searched. He was found to have 'a piece of Iron sharped at the one end' and was placed in a cell, following which two additional knives, 'sharped at the point as if for some desperate purpose', were discovered.[105]

With Erskine's intervention and the discovery of Linn's weapons the plot was quickly and quietly foiled. But it was clearly viewed as a serious matter, for several days later, on 13 February, two members of the gaol's board of superintendence, William Burleigh and Edward Bruce, conducted an investigation, taking statements, under oath, from the gaol's governor, James Erskine, and deputy keeper, Robert Forbes, and from four prisoners – John Crossan, Michael Walter Cash, Bernard McAnnaly and Patrick McMillan.[106] These statements reveal the extent of the plot, and something of its character. John Crossan, for instance, gave evidence that the 'conspiracy was entered into by almost all the Pris[oner]s in the class where he was confined' – that is, the crown class – and that it involved over fifty inmates.[107] Cash, McAnnally and McMillan likewise indicated that the plot concerned the crown prisoners, with McMillan claiming that it had involved 'the greater part of the Prisoners in the Crown Yard'; clearly, the conspiracy was an extensive one.[108] It was also an ecumenical one, involving both Catholic and Protestant inmates. Crossan revealed that those privy to the plot were sworn into it, and that the arrangements for this were determined by confessional allegiance. 'The agreement', he claimed, 'was for James Quinn to swear all the Catholic Prisoners on a manual and John Linn to swear the others on a Bible.'[109] The swearing-in of participants may be read as evidence of the conspirators' seriousness of intent, and further evidence on this score can be found in McMillan's recollection that he had 'heard it agreed and finally settled that James Colvin should be a leader and go to the female ward door [on the night of the escape] and keep the matrons inside to prevent alarm being given at the Barracks and bringing the soldiers down upon them'.[110] In a similar vein, Crossan explained that a prisoner named John Montague was tasked with destroying 'all the books and papers he could get hold of in order to prevent the Prisoners' descriptions being published in the Hue and Cry that would effect their escape'.[111]

In all of this, there is evidence of planning and determination. But what emerges most clearly from the evidence gathered by Burleigh and Bruce is the scale of the violence the conspiring prisoners planned to unleash, and the centrality to the plot of John Linn. Those involved in the plot swore 'to aid and assist each other in making their escape … and to fight each unto death rather than be prevented accomplishing their design', and it was intended that the escape would begin with the killing of the gaol's deputy keeper, Robert Forbes.[112] Linn undertook to carry out this attack, and evidently did so with some enthusiasm. While Crossan gave evidence that 'John Linn swore he would down Robert Forbes and put him from ever telling any tidings at the first part of the attack', Michael Cash related 'that he heard John Linn say … he would do for little Bobby' and Bernard McAnnaly recalled a disturbing conversation during which Linn, and a fellow conspirator, one James Quinn, discussed the projected murder: 'he heard John Linn swearing by Jesus he would pin Bobby (meaning Robert Forbes). James Quinn also said at the same time by Heavens if you miss him I'll hit him. Linn said there was no danger for I have as much about me as will clear the way.'[113]

Why Linn should have exhibited such a particular determination to kill Forbes is unclear, but there is evidence to suggest that he was a man who bore grudges. Reporting on the escape attempt on 8 February 1838, the *Northern Whig* reported that Linn had earlier 'made the most solemn asseverations ... that, if he ever escaped, he would undoubtedly murder the Proprietor of *The Whig*, for having published such a description of his person, as probably led to his detection [following his escape from the lunatic asylum]'.[114] Had Linn come, in a similar way, to develop a murderous hatred of Forbes? Was Forbes particularly officious in the discharge of his duties, or had he, at some point, slighted Linn? We will never know the answer to these questions, but we do know that the two men interacted. Indeed, in the statement he gave to Bruce and Burleigh on 13 February 1838, Forbes recalled an early encounter which offered a chilling insight into Linn's mindset:

> John Linn stated most distinctly to him the evening he was committed to said Gaol [i.e., Carrickfergus] from Kilmainham that no matter how many he killed the Law could take no hold of him as he was considered insane and unaccountable for any act he would commit.[115]

Forbes' testimony here aligns with that of Michael Cash, who asserted that 'Linn has stated to him that he being committed as a Lunatic might with impunity murder all the persons in the Gaol as the Law could not take hold of him'.[116] Having earlier railed against his treatment, it appears that Linn had perceived an opportunity in his classification as insane, and had come to believe that he could, quite literally, get away with murder.

He was, of course, incorrect. Had the escape plot continued without interruption, and had Forbes been killed, Linn would no doubt have faced a second murder trial – assuming, that is, he was recaptured. As it was, the conspiracy was thwarted, and on 15 March 1838 he was tried at the Antrim assizes on a charge of administering unlawful oaths.[117] The decision to press this charge was carefully arrived at. Having investigated the conspiracy on behalf of the gaol's board of superintendence, Edward Bruce and William Burleigh wrote to Dublin Castle, enclosing the statements of the prisoners and prison officers they had interviewed, along with 'three certificates' asserting that Linn was sane.[118] This material crossed the desk of Thomas Drummond, who had replaced William Gosset as under-secretary in July 1835, and who forwarded it to John Hamilton, the crown solicitor for the North East, in order 'that he may obtain the directions of the Attorney General with respect to the prosecution of the parties concerned in the Conspiracy and especially of Linn.'[119] Drummond's own view was clear. 'It would be very desirable', he noted of Linn, 'to have this man transported.'[120] The question, though, was how best to achieve this. When the attorney general's advice was sought, the complexities of the case were outlined:

> If the persons charged are indicted for the conspiracy to break the Gaol and are found guilty the offence being a misdemeanour only it is submitted that the punishment will not be commensurate with the offence imputed to the ringleaders of the party who appear to be indictable for the felonies, viz conspiracy to murder and the administering and taking unlawful oaths, being convicted on either of these charges it will be competent to the [court] to transport them.[121]

What charge should, then, be pressed, conspiracy to murder, or administering and taking unlawful oaths? On 21 February, the attorney general stated his opinion:

> the Prisoner Lynn should be prosecuted and such others of the prisoners as the Magistrates and Board of Superintendence think most culpable … they should be indicted for taking and administering unlawful oaths. Should the prosecution by any accident fail indictments for a conspiracy to break Prison should be preferred. I don't think an indictment for conspiracy to murder could be maintained.[122]

In the event, there was no need to make use of indictments for the lesser charge of conspiracy to escape. When brought to trial Linn was successfully prosecuted for administering unlawful oaths, receiving a sentence of seven years' transportation, and it was not necessary to prosecute the other leaders of the conspiracy, 'in as much as, each of them was convicted for the felony, for which he had been committed; and being so, was sentenced to a term of transportation respectively, beyond that of seven years – the statutable punishment for the administering & taking of unlawful oaths.'[123]

In the interactions of Drummond, Hamilton and the attorney general we can see the wheels of government efficiently turning, and the quiet preparations that were made to ensure that the problem of John Linn was dealt with once and for all. Given this, it is difficult to view the outcome of his final trial as anything other than inevitable. Yet it did offer some moments of drama and surprise. Silent during his trial for murder in 1833, Linn was vocal in March 1838. He represented himself during the proceedings, 'and every individual in a crowded Court, manifested the greatest astonishment at the remarkably able and astute manner in which he conducted his case'.[124] John Crossan, the chief witness for the prosecution, was no doubt particularly surprised when he found himself questioned 'at great length' by the very man against whom he was giving evidence. When this questioning 'elicited nothing material', Linn made his one significant throw of the dice, attempting to disrupt proceedings by protesting 'that he had been refused a copy of the information that had been made against him.' His stratagem did not succeed. James Erskine, the governor of Carrickfergus gaol, was on hand to clarify 'that every facility was afforded to

[the] prisoner to make his defence', and that he had been supplied with 'paper, ink, &c.' and informed that 'there were upwards of forty persons who had heard of the conspiracy'. Thereafter, the trial proceeded without particular incident, though it is apparent that the prosecution sought not only to establish Linn's involvement in the escape plot, but to determine his sanity. To this end, Robert Stuart, manager of the Belfast Lunatic Asylum, testified that he believed Linn 'to be of perfectly sane mind, as much so as any person in Court', and that he had 'never considered him to be insane'. There is a sense here of loose ends being tidied and of the path being cleared for the jury to arrive at a guilty verdict without niggling doubts about sanity and responsibility – and this it did. The trial culminated in a verdict of guilty, and Linn was sentenced to seven years' transportation.[125]

Sentence was not enforced immediately, but Linn did not have too long to wait. On 27 April 1838 he was committed to Kilmainhman Gaol in Dublin – most likely having spent the intervening period in Carrickfergus – and four days later, on 1 May 1838, he boarded the convict ship *Clyde*.[126] Evidently unaware of the full details of Linn's story, the *Clyde*'s surgeon, John Smith, baulked at his presence and 'made objection as believing him, from all I could learn of him, to be insane'.[127] But there was to be no last minute reprieve for Linn. The *Clyde* set sail on 11 May, and several months later, on 10 September 1838, at around midday, Linn and his fellow transportees arrived in Port Jackson, New South Wales. Five days later, they disembarked, mustered and began their new lives as convicts.[128]

Conclusion

With the arrival of the *Clyde* in New South Wales John Linn's story comes to an end, for nothing is known of his life in Australia.[1] But it is possible, in closing, to say something about his Irish afterlife. A figure as notorious as Linn was not easily forgotten, and his infamy lived on long after his departure from Ireland. Thus, in May 1839, the Ordnance Survey memoirist for Carrickfergus made reference to Linn in a brief account of the Carrickfergus escape conspiracy, patched together from information supplied by James Erskine, the gaol's governor, 'and many others'. The details given were somewhat garbled, suggesting that Linn had been 'convicted for the murder of his father' and had plotted escape while awaiting transportation, but what is significant is that Linn's story was being repeated and passed on.[2] In a similar vein, consider the following short report, which appeared in the *Northern Whig*, on 30 July 1839:

> It has been stated to us, that Linn, of Belfast, the notorious parricide, attempted to get up a mutiny in the ship in which he was sent, as a convict to New South Wales; and that he was tried, and shot, together with four or five of his accomplices.[3]

Had it been true, this would have provided a neat ending to Linn's story. As it was, it was entirely without foundation, and within days a correction had been published, which conceded 'that the report of the death of Linn was incorrect' and clarified that he had 'arrived safely at his destination, in New South Wales'.[4] What is striking, however, is that this story was told, and that it was judged plausible and considered newsworthy: clearly, Linn remained a subject of some interest.

Further evidence of continued interest in Linn and his story can be seen in an account of the Belfast quarter sessions that appeared in the *Northern Whig* late in October 1839. Reporting that John Crossan had been found guilty of the theft, the previous July, of a chair, the paper noted that he was an 'accomplice of Linn, the parricide'.[5] In reality, Crossan's relationship with Linn was more complicated: it was thanks in no small part to information he had provided that the Carrickfergus escape conspiracy was foiled, and he was a key witness for the prosecution at Linn's trial for administering unlawful oaths in March 1838.[6] For the *Northern Whig*, however, what mattered was that he could be connected with Linn, whose story remained fresh in the mind.

But beyond simply remembering it, contemporaries also sought to make use of Linn's story. Writing in 1851, Andrew Malcolm, the early chronicler of Belfast's medical institutions, gave a short but informed account of 'that notorious parricide, John Lynn', tying his case to the emergence of a campaign for the establishment of '*separate Criminal* Lunatic Asylums' that resulted, in 1850, in the opening of the Central Criminal Lunatic Asylum in Dundrum.[7] 'Stimulated by the circumstances of this and similar subsequent cases', Malcolm explained, 'the governors [of the Belfast Lunatic Asylum], year after year, carried on the agitation, in order to prevail upon the government to provide for criminal lunatics, and at last had the happiness of seeing the evil remedied by the passing of a special Act (the 8th and 9th Victoria, 1845), for the establishment of a central Asylum for insane persons charged with offences in Ireland.'[8]

How influential this agitation was is open to question, but it may well have played an indirect role in shaping policy, for Pauline Prior has traced the origins of the criminal asylum in Dundrum to the deliberations of the Select Committee on the State of the Lunatic Poor in Ireland, established in 1843, noting that the committee was 'influenced by the evidence presented by Dr Francis White, inspector of prisons' and that White 'had received complaints from managers of prisons and asylums about the presence of criminal lunatics in their institutions'.[9] Moreover, it is clear that the significance of Linn's story to wider debates regarding the management of criminal lunatics – and, an important distinction, criminals who *claimed* to be lunatics – was recognized in Belfast. Thus the Belfast Lunatic Asylum's *Eighth annual report*, covering the period April 1837 to March 1838, referred directly to the problems caused by 'the compulsory admission, from time to time, of criminals, stated to be lunatics, who have been acquitted of capital offences ... but who, almost invariably, prove, on transmission to the Asylum, to be in the perfect enjoyment of their mental faculties', citing Linn, 'the notorious parricide', as an example.[10] On 12 June 1838, these passages were brought to wider attention when they were republished in the *Northern Whig*, alongside commentary on the Dangerous Lunatic Act, which was then passing through parliament and which would, it was feared, lead to prisoners 'stated to be Lunatics' being moved from Ireland's gaols to its asylums.[11] Insofar as it illustrated the conceptual slipperiness of criminal insanity, and the extent to which it could be used to subvert the working of justice, Linn's case was viewed as relevant to these wider debates. As the *Northern Whig* observed, when commenting on a subsequent report from the Belfast Lunatic Asylum, Linn 'was no more insane than any other of those bad characters whose abandonment to vice leads them to the commission of the most atrocious crimes, and who might equally well escape the consequences thereof, by too indulgent Judges and Juries believing that they laboured under aberration of mind'.[12]

That Linn should have appeared, in this way, in the report of the Belfast Lunatic Asylum and the columns of the *Northern Whig* is scarcely surprising. His story was, after all, closely connected with that of the lunatic asylum during the period 1833–5, and the editor of the *Northern Whig* had taken a particular interest in his case, commenting on his character on a number of occasions following his escape from the asylum. There is, however, evidence to suggest that he was more widely remembered long after his departure from Ireland. In May 1862, Belfast was rocked by the murder of John Herdman, 'one of the wealthiest and most respectable manufacturers in the province'.[13] Herdman was killed by his cousin, William Herdman, who was tried in July 1862, and the following month an article on the case appeared in the *Ulster Magazine and Monthly Review of Science and Literature*.[14] Expressing satisfaction that serious crime was comparatively rare in Belfast, the author of the article noted that:

> It is now more than thirty years since the name of Belfast has been stained with the commission of a crime so awful as that of murder. The last occasion on which life was taken away by violence was that of an infuriated son destroying his venerable father in an impulse of passion. It was shown upon his trial that the delinquent had never been of sound intellect, and the jury declined to convict. It is not necessary to specify the name of either the criminal or the victim in this case. Both are well remembered.[15]

In some respects, these comments were poorly informed. The citizens of Belfast did not need to look back thirty years to find a shocking example of murder: just twelve years previously, in December 1850, a Belfast mill worker named John M'Manus had killed his father in Wylie's Place, in what was reported, by the *Northern Whig*, as a 'Frightful Case of Parricide'.[16] Nevertheless, it was the earlier Linn murder that had stuck in the writer's mind – a murder so notorious that some thirty years after the act it could be alluded to obliquely, in full confidence that readers could identify the 'venerable father' and 'infuriated son' as William and John Linn.

Later still, Linn made a brief appearance in Thomas Gaffikin's *Belfast fifty years ago*. First published in 1875, this valuable account of early 19th-century Belfast was republished in expanded form in 1885 and 1894, and it was in the expanded edition that Gaffikin made reference to Linn.[17] Recalling the political and confessional tensions of an earlier age, Gaffikin explained that:

> The Liberals and Conservatives, or rather the Catholics and Orangmen, became pitted against each other. John M'Clean, the Catholic champion, and his party would attack the Orangemen on a July anniversary. John Lynn, again – better known as 'Lippy Lynn' – defended the Orangemen as their champion; and pitched battles and skirmishing were kept up for a considerable time, especially during Parliamentary elections, which sometimes lasted a whole week.[18]

What is striking here, of course, is that no mention is made of the more dramatic aspects of Linn's story. He is presented simply as a street-fighter – a colourful figure to rank alongside the fiddle-player Cockeybendy, Tantra Barbus 'who would have danced for buttons' and the other 'street celebrities' that appear earlier in the narrative.[19] Why Gaffikin should have chosen to present Linn in this way is unclear. That he was unaware of Linn's murder of his father seems unlikely, though it is possible that he avoided reference to it in deference to his sensibilities. Although happy to allude to the darker side of urban life, in the form of passing references to public floggings, cock-fighting, duelling and executions, Gaffikin perhaps considered the detailed discussion of an individual parricide, and the family tragedy it entailed, to be another matter entirely.[20] Alternatively, practical considerations might have induced him to overlook the events of 29 August 1832, and their protracted aftermath: where Linn the street-fighter was a colourful personality, who could easily be mentioned in passing, Linn the murderer was an altogether different figure, whose troubling story could not easily be dealt with in the relaxed, anecdotal style Gaffikin employed. But whatever the explanation, Linn did not appear in this evidently popular text – it was reprinted in 1894 'in response to repeated inquiries' – as a murderer, asylum escapee, would-be gaol-breaker or transportee. He appeared simply as a Belfast brawler.[21] His story had begun to fragment, and in the years that followed he, and it, passed from memory.

* * *

What, then, should we make of the story of John Linn? Or to put this another way, what is its significance? One answer to this question has been provided by Richard Cobb, the innovative and unconventional historian of Revolutionary France.[22] Questioned as to the 'historical relevance' of his account of 'L'Affaire Perken', a double murder which occurred in the Dutch hamlet of Notendaal in 1809, Cobb's response was that 'it was something that happened at a given place in a given period; and as the account of it, from start to finish, was remarkably complete, it appeared to me to be worth telling', and he later observed that 'a continued insistence on relevance would soon result in the abandonment of the study of the past and the end of history as we know it, that is as a cultural subject, enriching in itself'.[23] But if we might, echoing Cobb, conclude that stories such as Linn's are worth reconstructing on their own terms, we can also go further. Taking us from the streets of Belfast to the decks of the *Clyde*, via the courtroom, the lunatic asylum and the county gaol, Linn's story is a revealing and multifaceted one. It is a story that takes us beyond population statistics and clichés about confessional violence, offering a revealing glimpse of the experience of one working-class Belfast family in a period of rapid urban expansion. In many respects a family tragedy, Linn's story is one in which we see upward social mobility violently frustrated, and three small children – the grandchildren of a respectable artisan – reduced to the Belfast Poor House. It is the story, too, of a deformed child – Linn himself – who made a name for himself with his fists, becoming a Belfast 'hard man', and a story that offers an intriguing sidelight on the growth of the state, in the form of the dispute that emerged between the lord lieutenant and the governors of the Belfast Lunatic Asylum as to where Linn should be confined. But above all, following Linn's protracted journey through the courts and the carceral spaces of early 19th-century Ireland offers an intriguing view of the working of the criminal justice system – a view that reminds us that that system did not always function smoothly, and that it was, at times, susceptible to subversion. Judged insane in March 1833, Linn appears to have been anything but, and in the years that followed he exercised agency in a variety of ways, by petitioning the lord lieutenant, escaping from the lunatic asylum, plotting a murderous conspiracy in Carrickfergus gaol and representing himself in court. In the end, the problem of Linn was dealt with, and he was transported to New South Wales. The point, however, is that he had to be dealt with: Linn was, from March 1833, a recurrent problem, and if his story illustrates anything, it is that those who found themselves in the courts, prisons and asylums of 19th-century Ireland were not always passive recipients of the state's attempts to control and confine.

Notes

ABBREVIATIONS

BCC	*Belfast Commercial Chronicle*
BNL	*Belfast News-Letter*
DIB	*Dictionary of Irish biography: from the earliest times to the year 2002* (accessed online at https://dib.cambridge.org/)
Eighth annual report	*Eighth annual report, &c., of the Belfast District Asylum, for the Lunatic Poor of the counties of Antrim, Down, and county of the town of Carrickfergus, being from 1st April, 1837, till 31st March, 1838, submitted to the board of governors, by the managers* (Belfast, 1838) (PRONI, HOS/28/1/5/1)
FJ	*Freeman's Journal*
GCA	*Guardian and Constitutional Advocate*
Malcolm, *History*	A.G. Malcolm, *The history of the General Hospital, Belfast, and the other medical institutions of the town: with chronological notes & biographical reminiscences connected with its rise and progress* (Belfast, 1851)
NAI	National Archives of Ireland
NLA	National Library of Australia
NW	*Northern Whig*
PRONI	Public Record Office of Northern Ireland
R.C., 'Case'	R.C. 'Case of John Linn, a parricide', *The Phrenological Journal and Miscellany*, 10 (1836–7), 220–17

INTRODUCTION

1 In addition to the 215 convicts boarded in Dublin, a further 20 military convicts were boarded in late July 1838, when the *Clyde* called at the Cape Colony. 'Diary of occurrences on board the convict ship Clyde', pp 5, 7–8, 10–14, 21–2, 35–9 (NLA, MS 6169), available online at https://catalogue.nla.gov.au/ Record/2084065 (accessed 8 April 2020). Page numbers refer to online PDF; henceforth cited as 'Diary'.

2 *BNL*, 31 Aug. 1832; *BCC*, 1 Sept. 1832; R.C., 'Case', 209.

3 'Diary', p. 8.

4 *NW*, 30 Aug. 1832. See also *GCA* and *BNL*, 31 Aug. 1832; *BCC*, 1 Sept. 1832.

5 *GCA*, 19 March 1833; *NW*, 18 March 1833. See also, *BNL*, 19 March 1833.

6 *GCA*, 19 March 1833 and 24 Nov. 1835; *NW*, 26 Nov. 1835; *BNL*, 27 Nov. 1835.

7 *FJ*, 3 Sept. 1836. See also, *NW*, 5 Sept. 1836.

8 *FJ*, 3 Sept. 1836; *NW*, 12 Sept. 1836; 'Certificate of James Erskine Governor of Carrickfergus Gaol' (NAI, CRF 1838, Misc 10) (MFS/59/11).

9 *NW*, 8 Feb. 1838.

10 *BNL*, 16 March 1838; *NW*, 17 March 1838.

11 In addition to the newspaper reports cited above, see, for contemporary/near contemporary discussion of Linn's case: R.C., 'Case'; *Eighth annual report*, p. 7; Malcolm, *History*, pp 91–2.

12 Keith Haines, 'Carrickfergus gaol conspiracy 1838', *Due North*, 1 (Oct. 1999), 3–9; Jonathan Jeffrey Wright, 'Stranger than fiction: the story of John "Lippy" Linn' in Salvador Ryan (ed.), *Death and the Irish: a miscellany* (Dublin, 2016), pp 115–19.

13 A brief and inaccurate account of Linn's story can also, however, be found in [Department of Anatomy, University of Edinburgh], *Death masks and life masks of*

the famous and infamous: from the collections
in the University of Edinburgh's Department
of Anatomy (Edinburgh, 1988), p. 36.

14 R.C., 'Case'. Extracts from this account
have recently been reproduced in
Reggie Chamberlain-King, *Weird Belfast:
a miscellany, almanack and companion*
(Belfast, 2014), pp 83–7, though they
are presented without commentary, and
no attempt is made to contextualize or
analyse their content.

15 Arthur Deane (ed.), *The Belfast Natural
History and Philosophical Society. Centenary
volume, 1821–1921* (Belfast, 1924), p. 79;
R.C., 'Case', 207, 209–12, 213–15, 216.

16 Giovanni Levi, 'On microhistory' in
Peter Burke (ed.), *New perspectives on
historical writing* (Cambridge, 1991),
pp 93–113 at 93, 95, 97. See also, for a
more recent account of microhistory's
development, Sigurður Gylfi
Magnússon and István M. Szijártó,
What is microhistory?: Theory and practice
(Abingdon, 2013).

17 Gordon S. Wood, *The purpose of the past:
reflections on the uses of history* (New York,
2008), p. 127.

18 Ibid., pp 128–9. See also Richard J.
Evans, *Tales from the German underworld*
(New Haven, 1998), p. 4 and, for
criticism from a slightly different
direction, Jo Guldi and David Armitage,
The history manifesto (Cambridge, 2014),
pp 11, 45–6, 121.

19 See Emmanuel Le Roy Ladurie,
*Montaillou, Cathars and Catholics in
a French village, 1294–1324* (London,
1978); Natalie Zemon Davis, *The return
of Martin Guerre* (Cambridge, Mass.,
1983); Carlo Ginzburg, *The cheese and
the worms: the cosmos of a sixteenth-century
Miller* (Baltimore, 1992). Note though
that Davis has observed that 'I rarely
find myself thinking about whether I am
doing "macrohistory" or "microhistory"
at any given time. I simply feel I'm
doing history *tout court*'. See, Natalie
Zemon Davis, 'Martin Luther, Martin
Guerre, and ways of knowing', *Common
Knowledge*, 20 (2014), 4–8 at 6.

20 Edward Muir and Guido Ruggiero,
'Introduction' in Edward Muir and
Guido Ruggiero (eds), *History from crime*
(Baltimore, 1994), pp vii–xviii at viii.

21 Ibid., pp viii, ix. See also V.A.C. Gatrell,
*The hanging tree: execution and the English
people, 1770–1868* (Oxford, 1996), p. 448.

1. 'A YOUNG MAN OF UNGOVERNABLE
PASSIONS'

1 'Kilmainham Prison General Register
1835–1837 (Book No: 1/10/3)' entry
709 and 'Kilmainham Prison General
Register 1836–1840 (Book No: 1/10/3)'
entry 1399 (NAI, accessible via Find My
Past).

2 'Transportation Register Males and
Females 1837–8' (NAI, TR2) (MFS
56/10); 'John Lynn [Linn] Record
ID cin47776', available online at
https://www.digitalpanopticon.org/
life?id=cin47776 (accessed 7 Nov. 2019).

3 Raymond Gillespie and Stephen A.
Royle, *Belfast: part 1, to 1840* (Irish
Historic Towns Atlas) (Dublin, 2003),
p. 10; S.J. Connolly, 'Improving town,
1750–1820,' in S.J. Connolly (ed.), *Belfast
400: people, place and history* (Liverpool,
2012), pp 161–97 at 173.

4 *The Drennan–McTier Letters*, ed. Jean
Agnew (3 vols, Dublin, 1998–9), iii,
61.

5 Raymond Gillespie, *Early Belfast: the
origins and growth of an Ulster town to 1750*
(Belfast, 2007), p. 167; Jonathan Jeffrey
Wright, '"The Donegalls' backside":
Donegall Place, the White Linen Hall
and the development of space and
place in nineteenth-century Belfast'
in Georgina Laragy, Olwen Purdue
and Jonathan Jeffrey Wright (eds),
Urban spaces in nineteenth-century Ireland
(Liverpool, 2018), pp 61–83 at 62.

6 Jonathan Jeffrey Wright, *The 'natural
leaders' and their world: politics, culture and
society in Belfast, c.1801–1832* (Liverpool,
2012), chapter 5. For crime in Belfast,
see Brian Griffin, *The Bulkies: police and
crime in Belfast, 1800–1865* (Dublin, 1998),
especially chapter 5.

7 Thomas Bradshaw, *Belfast general &
commercial directory for 1819: containing
an alphabetical list of the merchants,
manufacturers, and inhabitants in general; and
a history of Belfast, and its institutions: with
a directory and history of Lisburn* (Belfast,
1819), p. 44.

8 *GCA* and *BNL*, 31 Aug. 1832.

9 J.R.R. Adams, *Merchants in plenty: Joseph Smyth's Belfast directories of 1807 and 1808* (Belfast, 1991), p. 26.

10 *BNL*, 16 May 1828; 'Register "C" Marriages 1810–1846', p. 126 (PRONI, T654/4).

11 R.C., 'Case', 213–14.

12 Ibid., 213.

13 *NW*, 2 March 1826; *BCC*, 1 Sept. 1832; *GCA*, 24 Nov. 1835; *BNL*, 27 Nov. 1835; R. C., 'Case', 209.

14 R.C., 'Case', 209.

15 Josip Bill, Peter Proff, Thomas Bayerlein, Jens Weingaertner, Jochen Fanghänel and Jürgen Reuther, 'Treatment of patients with cleft lip, alveolus and palate – a short outline of history and current interdisciplinary treatment approaches', *Journal of Cranio-Maxillofacial Surgery*, 34, Suppl. 2 (2006), 17–21 at 18; S. Bhattacharya, V. Khanna and R. Kohli, 'Cleft lip: the historical perspective', *Indian Journal of Plastic Surgery*, 42, Suppl. (2009), S4–S8, available online at https://www.ncbi.nlm.nih.gov/pmc/articles/PMC2825059/ (accessed 7 Jan. 2020) (quote from page 6 of online edition).

16 R.C., 'Case', 207, 209.

17 *BCC*, 1 Sept. 1832 (this report was reprinted in R.C., 'Case', 207–8, though it is misdated and the comment regarding Linn's nickname is rephrased and repositioned within the report). For further references to Linn's nickname, see *NW*, 2 March 1826; *BNL*, 3 March 1826.

18 Bradshaw, *Directory*, pp 130–2.

19 Wright, *The 'natural leaders'*, pp 226–7.

20 'The Petition of John Linn now confined in the Belfast District Lunatic Asylum' and 'The Petition of John Lynn … at present confined in Carrickfergus Gaol' (NAI, CRF 1837, Misc 5) (MFS/59/08); R.C., 'Case', 211.

21 *BNL*, 16 May 1828; George Benn, *The history of the town of Belfast, with an accurate account of its former & present state: to which are added a statistical survey of the parish of Belfast, and a description of some remarkable antiquities in its neighbourhood* (Belfast, 1823), p. 113; 'Register "C" Marriages 1810–1846', p. 126 (PRONI, T654/4); 'John Lynn [Linn] Record ID cin47776',

available online at https://www.digitalpanopticon.org/life?id=cin47776 (accessed 7 Nov. 2019).

22 *GCA* and *BNL*, 31 Aug. 1832; *BCC*, 1 Sept. 1832.

23 *BNL*, 2 Aug. 1825.

24 W.D. Killen, *History of congregations of the Presbyterian Church in Ireland and biographical notices of eminent Presbyterian ministers and laymen* (Belfast, 1886), pp 62–3, 259–60; R. Finlay Holmes, *Henry Cooke* (Belfast, 1981), p. 31 (and chapters 2 and 3 passim for the disputes of the 1820s).

25 R.C., 'Case', 210; Malcolm, *History*, p. 91.

26 Alister E. McGrath, *Christian theology: an introduction*, 2nd ed. (Oxford, 1997), p. 453.

27 'Pew transfer slip, 1839, of Francis McCracken' (PRONI, MIC1P/7/7); Mary McNeill, *The life and times of Mary Ann McCracken, 1770–1866: a Belfast panorama* (Belfast, 1988), p. 60.

28 McNeill, *Mary Ann McCracken*, pp 242–5. The exception was Mary Ann McCracken's brother John, whose business flourished in the early 19th century.

29 [PRONI], *Problems of a growing city: Belfast, 1780–1870* (Belfast, 1973), pp 89–90.

30 Ibid., pp 81–2.

31 *GCA*, 31 Aug. 1832.

32 *BNL*, 31 Aug. 1832.

33 Katie Barclay, *Men on trial: performing emotion, embodiment and identity in Ireland, 1800–45* (Manchester, 2019), p. 20; Andrew R. Holmes, *The shaping of Ulster Presbyterian belief and practice, 1770–1840* (Oxford, 2006), pp 66–9.

34 E.P. Thompson, *The making of the English working class* (London, 1974), p. 260; John Rule, *The labouring classes in early industrial England, 1750–1850* (London, 1986), pp 36–7.

35 *BCC*, 1 Sept. 1832; Bradshaw, *Directory*, p. 44.

36 R.C., 'Case', 209, 214.

37 *BNL*, 16 May 1828; *NW*, 22 May 1828.

38 R.C., 'Case', 214. See also, *NW*, 30 Aug. 1832.

39 Dominic Bryan and S. J. Connolly, with John Nagle, *Civic identity and public space:*

Belfast since 1780 (Manchester, 2019), pp 63–4; Gillespie and Royle, *Belfast*, p. 6 and maps 11 and 13; Gillespie, *Early Belfast*, pp 1–2, 173.

40 Derived from George Benn's 1823 history of Belfast, the figures given here do not include the population of the streets that bordered the Smithfield district to the north (North Street), south (Castle Street and Mill Street), east (Hercules Street) and west (Millfield). Nor do they include the population of Bank Lane or Millers Lane, which were located within the Smithfield quarter, but for which Benn does not give figures. Benn, *History of the town of Belfast*, pp 295–6; Gillespie and Royle, *Belfast*, p. 11.

41 Bradshaw, *Directory*, p. 44; *BNL*, 31 Aug. 1832.

42 Thomas Gaffikin, *Belfast fifty years ago. A lecture, delivered by Thomas Gaffikin, in the Working Men's Institute, Belfast on Thursday Evg., April 8th, 1875, James Alex. Henderson, Esq., J.P. (ex-mayor of Belfast), in the chair* (Belfast, 1894), pp 28–9.

43 [Anon.], *The 'Northern Athens'; or, life in the Emerald Isle. A socio-comico-ludicro-satiric poem* (Belfast, 1826), p. 26.

44 Keith Haines, 'Carrickfergus gaol conspiracy 1838', *Due North*, 1 (Oct. 1999), 3–9 at 3–4.

45 W.M. O'Hanlon, *Walks among the poor of Belfast, and suggestions for their improvement* (Belfast, 1853), p. 42.

46 Ibid., pp 43–5, 48.

47 Gillespie and Royle, *Belfast*, pp 8–9; Stephen A. Royle, 'The socio-spatial structure of Belfast in 1837: evidence from the first valuation', *Irish Geography*, 24 (1991), 1–9 at 5.

48 Royle, 'Socio-spatial structure', 8.

49 Gaffikin, *Belfast fifty years ago*, p. 28; O'Hanlon, *Walks*, pp 38, 43.

50 *Charles Abbot's tour through Ireland and North Wales in September and October 1792*, ed. C.J. Woods (Dublin, 2019), p. 32.

51 S.J. Connolly and Gillian McIntosh, 'Whose city? Belonging and exclusion in the nineteenth-century urban world' in Connolly (ed.), *Belfast 400*, pp 237–69 at 245–6; Royle, 'Socio-spatial structure', 8; Fred Heatley, 'Community relations and the religious geography 1800–86' in

J.C. Beckett et al., *Belfast: the making of the city* (Belfast, 2008), pp 129–42 at 131, 133–4. See also, Ian Budge and Cornelius O'Leary, *Belfast: approach to crisis: a study of Belfast politics, 1613–1970* (London, 1973), pp 31–3; Sean Farrell, *Rituals and riots: sectarian violence and political culture in Ulster, 1784–1886* (Lexington, KY, 2000), pp 127, 135.

52 Gillespe and Royle, *Belfast*, pp 8–9. See also Farrell, *Rituals and riots*, pp 135–6.

53 *NW*, 14 July 1825; Budge and O'Leary, *Belfast: approach to crisis*, pp 23, 25; Farrell, *Rituals and riots*, pp 80–1.

54 David W. Miller (ed.), *Peep O'Day Boys and Defenders: selected documents on the County Armagh disturbances, 1784–96* (Belfast, 1990); Farrell, *Rituals and riots*, pp 10–31, 35–46. For Orangeism in early 19th-century Belfast see, Budge and O'Leary, *Belfast: approach to crisis*, p. 24; Catherine Hirst, *Religion, politics and violence in nineteenth-century Belfast: the Pound and Sandy Row* (Dublin, 2002), p. 23.

55 Samuel M'Skimin, *Annals of Ulster; or, Ireland fifty years ago* (Belfast, 1849), pp 53, 89.

56 *Drennan–McTier Letters*, ed. Agnew, iii, 56.

57 [Anon.], *Trial of the Belfast Orangemen* (Belfast, 1813), pp 4–7; Wright, *The 'natural leaders'*, pp 80–1; Farrell, *Riots and rituals*, pp 32–3; Hirst, *Religion, politics and violence*, pp 20–1, 29; Budge and O'Leary, *Belfast: approach to crisis*, pp 24–5; Connolly and McIntosh, 'Whose city?', p. 245.

58 *The Irishman*, 11 July 1823.

59 *BNL*, 15 July 1823.

60 *BNL*, 13 July 1824.

61 *NW*, 14 July 1825. The events of 12 July 1825 have been discussed in brief in Budge and O'Leary, *Belfast: approach to crisis*, p. 25 and Hirst, *Religion, politics and violence*, p. 29.

62 *NW*, 14 July 1825.

63 *BNL*, 15 July 1825; *NW*, 14 July 1825.

64 *NW*, 14 July 1825.

65 *BNL*, 15 July 1825.

66 *NW*, 14 and 21 July 1825; *BNL*, 15 and 29 July 1825.

67 *BNL*, 29 July and 2 Aug. 1825; *NW*, 4 Aug. 1825.

68 *BNL*, 2 Aug. 1825.
69 Ibid.
70 *BNL*, 15 July 1825.
71 [Anon.], *The 'Northern Athens'*, pp 37, 40, 41, 42.
72 Ibid., pp 39–40.
73 R.C., 'Case', 209.
74 Ibid.; *BNL*, 31 Aug. 1832.
75 *BNL*, 2 Aug. 1825 and 28 March 1826 (M'Lean is here given as M'Lain); *NW*, 30 March 1826.
76 *BNL*, 28 March 1826.
77 *BNL*, 2 Aug. 1825.
78 Gaffikin, *Belfast fifty years ago*, p. 41 (M'Lean is given here as M'Clean).
79 Sean O'Connell, 'Violence and social memory in twentieth-century Belfast: stories of Buck Alec Robinson', *Journal of British Studies*, 53 (2014), 734–56 at 734, 735, 737, 743.
80 *NW*, 2 March 1826.
81 Ibid.; Barclay, *Men on trial*, p. 42.
82 Barclay, *Men on trial*, pp 3, 5.
83 Ibid., pp 97, 99.
84 *NW*, 2 March 1826.

2. 'HORRID MURDER. – PARRICIDE.'

1 *BNL*, 28 March 1826; *NW*, 30 March 1826.
2 *NW*, 30 March 1826.
3 *NW*, 30 Aug. 1832 and 18 March 1833; 'The Petition of John Linn now confined in the Belfast District Lunatic Asylum' (NAI, CRF 1837, Misc 5) (MFS/59/08); 'Committee Book' of the Belfast Charitable Society, entry for 7 June 1834 (PRONI, MIC61/6); 'Registry Book' of Clifton Street Cemetery, pp 12, 20, available online at http://www.belfasthistoryproject.com/cliftonstreetcemetery/ (accessed 1 Sept. 2019).
4 *BCC*, 1 Sept. 1832; *NW*, 18 March 1833.
5 R.C., 'Case', 215.
6 'Certificate of James Erskine Governor of Carrickfergus Gaol' (NAI, CRF 1838, Misc 10) (MFS/59/11).
7 *BNL*, 31 Aug. 1832; *BCC*, 1 Sept. 1832.
8 *BCC*, 1 Sept. 1832; *NW*, 18 March 1833.
9 *BCC*, 1 Sept. 1832; *NW*, 18 March 1833.
10 *NW*, 30 Aug. 1832.
11 *BNL*, 31 Aug. 1832.
12 R.C., 'Case', 209.
13 Ibid., 212–13.
14 Ibid., 214 (emphasis added).
15 Ibid., 214.
16 Ibid., 210.
17 *GCA*, 31 Aug. 1832.
18 'Certificate of James Erskine Governor of Carrickfergus Gaol' (NAI, CRF 1838, Misc 10) (MFS/59/11).
19 *NW*, 18 March 1833.
20 Ibid.
21 *BNL*, 31 Aug. 1832; *BCC*, 1 Sept. 1832.
22 *BNL*, 31 Aug. 1832; *BCC*, 1 Sept. 1832.
23 *BNL*, 31 Aug. 1832; *BCC*, 1 Sept. 1832;
24 *BCC*, 1 Sept. 1832; *BNL*, 19 March 1833.
25 *BNL*, 31 Aug. 1832.
26 Edward Muir and Guido Ruggiero, 'Introduction' in Edward Muir and Guido Ruggiero (eds), *History from crime* (Baltimore, 1994), pp vii–xviii at viii.
27 *BNL*, 31 Aug. 1832; *BCC*, 1 Sept. 1832.
28 Richard Mc Mahon, *Homicide in pre-Famine and Famine Ireland* (Liverpool, 2017), pp 1–4, 12–31 (30 and 31 for quotes).
29 Ibid., pp 23–5, 28.
30 *GCA*, 19 March 1833.
31 Ian Budge and Cornelius O'Leary, *Belfast: approach to crisis: a study of Belfast politics, 1613–1970* (London, 1973), p. 43; Raymond Gillespie and Stephen A. Royle, *Belfast: part 1, to 1840* (Irish Historic Towns Atlas) (Dublin, 2003), p. 9.
32 [Anon.], *Trial of the Belfast Orangemen* (Belfast, 1813), p. 28.
33 Catherine Hirst, *Religion, politics and violence in nineteenth-century Belfast: the Pound and Sandy Row* (Dublin, 2002), p. 32; *BNL*, 20 April 1832.
34 *NW*, 6 Nov. 1828; *BNL*, 31 March 1829.
35 *BNL*, 27 April and 28 Aug. 1810; George Benn, *A history of the town of Belfast from 1799 till 1810 together with some incidental notices on local topics and biographies of many well-known families* (London, 1880), p. 78.
36 *BNL*, 20 April 1832; *NW*, 4 Sept. 1832.
37 *BNL*, 31 Aug. 1832; *GCA*, 31 Aug. 1832.
38 *GCA*, 31 Aug. 1832; *BCC*, 1 Sept. 1832.
39 *BNL*, 31 Aug. 1832.
40 *GCA* and *BNL*, 31 Aug. 1832; *BCC*, 1 Sept. 1832.
41 *NW*, 30 Aug. 1832
42 *GCA* and *BNL*, 31 Aug. 1832.
43 *BCC*, 1 Sept. 1832.
44 *NW*, 30 Aug. 1832.

45 *GCA*, 31 Aug. 1832.

46 Wright, *The 'natural leaders'*, pp 57, 124.

47 Mc Mahon, *Homicide*, p. 75n62.

48 Ann-Marie Kilday, '"Sugar and spice and all things nice?": Violence against parents in Scotland, 1700–1850', *Journal of Family History*, 41 (2016), 318–35 at 331.

49 Garthine Walker, 'Imagining the unimaginable: parricide in early modern England and Wales, *c.*1600–*c.*1760', *Journal of Family History*, 41 (2016), 271–93 at 272, 273.

50 Michel Foucault (ed.), *I, Pierre Rivière, having slaughtered my mother my sister, and my brother... a case of parricide in the nineteenth century* (New York, 1975), pp 16–18, 54. See also the essays on Rivière collected in *Emotion Space Society*, 5 (2012), 207–78.

51 *BNL*, 12 and 15 Feb. 1811.

52 *BNL*, 23 Dec. 1817 and 20 Jan., 31 Aug. and 14 Dec. 1824.

53 *BNL*, 27 Jan. 1818 and 1 April 1828. See also, *BNL*, 5 Oct. 1813, 1 and 8 July 1823 and 4 July 1826.

54 *BNL*, 29 Jan. 1828.

55 *BNL*, 23 April 1816 and 25 March 1817.

56 *BNL*, 23 April 1816 and 25 March 1817.

57 *BNL*, 25 March 1817. W.E. Vaughan, *Murder trials in Ireland, 1836–1914* (Dublin, 2009), p. 293.

58 *BNL*, 28 March 1817.

59 *Newry Magazine; Or, Literary & Political Register*, 3 (1817), 164; *Blackwood's Edinburgh Magazine*, 1 (1817), 324; *Anti-Jacobin Review*, 52 (1817), 289–97, 388–92.

60 Emily Lorraine de Montluzin, *The anti-Jacobins, 1798–1800: the early contributors to the 'Anti-Jacobin Review'* (Basingstoke, 1988), pp 93, 94.

61 *Anti-Jacobin Review*, 52 (1817), 392.

62 Ibid., 391–2.

63 *BNL*, 28 March 1817.

64 Gillespie and Royle, *Belfast*, p. 22 and map 11; George Benn, *The history of the town of Belfast, with an accurate account of its former & present state: to which are added a statistical survey of the parish of Belfast, and a description of some remarkable antiquities in its neighbourhood* (Belfast, 1823), p. 108; C.E.B. Brett, *Buildings of Belfast, 1700–1914*, revised edition (Belfast, 1985), p. 15; Thomas Gaffikin, *Belfast fifty years ago. A lecture, delivered by Thomas Gaffikin,* in the Working Men's Institute, Belfast on Thursday Evg., April 8th, 1875, James Alex. Henderson, Esq., J.P. (ex-mayor of Belfast), in the chair (Belfast, 1894), p. 16.

65 *BCC*, 1 Sept. 1832; James Adair Pilson, *History of the rise and progress of Belfast, and annals of the County Antrim, from the earliest period to the present time* (Belfast, 1846), p. 184.

66 Brian Griffin, *The Bulkies: police and crime in Belfast, 1800–1865* (Dublin, 1998), pp 5, 18.

67 Ibid., pp 18, 24–5, 51; *BNL*, 16 Jan. 1827.

68 [PRONI], *Problems of a growing city: Belfast, 1780–1870* (Belfast, 1973), pp 1, 3.

69 *GCA* and *BNL*, 31 Aug. 1832; *BCC*, 1 Sept. 1832, *NW*, 18 March 1833.

70 *GCA*, 31 Aug. 1832; *BCC*, 1 Sept. 1832.

71 *BCC*, 1 Sept. 1832, *NW*, 18 March 1833.

72 *BCC*, 1 Sept. 1832.

73 *BCC*, 31 Sept. 1832. See also *NW*, 30 Aug. 1832; *BNL*, 31 Aug. 1832.

74 *GCA* and *BNL*, 31 Aug. 1832; *BCC*, 1 Sept. 1832.

75 *GCA*, 31 Aug. 1832; *BCC*, 1 Sept. 1832; Gillespie and Royle, *Belfast*, p. 22; Griffin, *The Bulkies*, pp 41–2.

76 Vaughan, *Murder trials*, p. 47.

77 *NW*, 30 Aug. 1832; *GCA* and *BNL*, 31 Aug. 1832.

78 *NW*, 30 Aug. 1832; *BCC*, 1 Sept. 1832.

79 Vaughan, *Murder trials*, p. 40.

80 *BCC*, 1 Sept. 1832.

81 Vaughan, *Murder trials*, p. 41; *GCA*, 31 Aug. 1832. See also, *BCC*, 1 Sept. 1832.

82 Vaughan, *Murder trials*, pp 4, 86.

83 Ibid., p. 89.

84 *BNL*, 15 March 1833; F. Elrington Ball, *The judges in Ireland, 1221–1921*, vol. ii (New York, 1927), p. 342.

85 *BNL*, 15 and 19 March 1833. For Finlay, see Patrick M. Geoghegan, 'Finlay, Francis Dalzell' in *DIB*.

86 *BNL*, 19 March 1833.

87 Ibid. See also *GCA*, 19 March 1833 and *NW*, 18 March 1833.

88 *NW*, 2 March 1826.

89 *Eighth annual report*, p. 7.

90 *NW*, 18 March 1833.

91 Ibid.; *BNL* and *GCA*, 19 March 1833.

92 *NW*, 30 Aug. 1832.

93 *BNL*, 31 Aug. 1832.

94 Catherine L. Evans, 'At her majesty's pleasure: criminal insanity in 19th-

century Britain', *History Compass*, 14 (2016), 470–9 at 471.

95 Brendan D. Kelly, 'Criminal insanity in 19th-century Ireland, Europe, and the United States: cases, contexts and controversies', *International Journal of Law and Psychiatry*, 32 (2009), 362–8 at 363–4 (363 for quote); Vaughan, *Murder trials*, pp 20–1; Evans, 'At her majesty's pleasure', 473; Pauline Prior, 'Dangerous lunacy: the misuse of mental health law in nineteenth-century Ireland', *Journal of Forensic Psychiatry*, 14 (2003), 525–41. See also, Walker, 'Imagining the unimaginable', 274–5 and, for the Dangerous Lunatics Act, Oonagh Walsh, 'Lunatics and criminal alliances in nineteenth-century Ireland' in Peter Bartlett and David Wright (eds), *Outside the walls of the asylum: the history of care in the community, 1750–2000* (London, 1999), pp 132–52 at 134–5; Catherine Cox, *Negotiating insanity in the southeast of Ireland, 1820–1900* (Manchester, 2012), pp 76–7.

96 Walker, 'Imagining the unimaginable,' 275.

97 Alannah Hopkin, with Kathy Bunney, *The ship of seven murders: a true story of madness and murder* (Cork, 2010), pp 1–6, 151–2, 177–8, 198 (177 for quote). See also, Helena Kelleher Kahn, '"Forced from this world": massacre on the *Mary Russell*', *History Ireland*, 17 (Sept./Oct. 2009), 22–6.

98 Hopkin, with Bunney, *Ship of seven murders*, pp 2–3, 86, 90–3, 103–4 106.

99 Ibid., pp 152, 180.

100 *BNL*, 1 and 4 July 1828.

101 *BNL*, 15 Aug. 1828.

102 *NW*, 18 March 1833; *BNL* and *GCA*, 19 March 1833.

103 Mc Mahon, *Homicide*, pp 34, 39–40, 71; Vaughan, *Murder trials*, p. 321; Pauline M. Prior, 'Murder and madness: gender and the insanity defence in nineteenth-century Ireland', *New Hibernia Review*, 9 (Winter, 2005), 19–36 at 31. See also, Pauline Prior, 'Roasting a man alive: the case of Mary Reilly, criminal lunatic', *Éire-Ireland*, 41 (Spring/Summer, 2006), 169–91 at 177, 186, 189.

104 *BNL*, 31 Aug. 1832; *NW*, 18 March 1833.

105 *BCC*, 1 Sept. 1832; *NW*, 18 March 1833.

106 *NW*, 18 March 1833.

107 Ibid.; *BNL* and *GCA*, 19 March 1833.

108 *NW*, 18 March 1833.

109 Quoted in Vaughan, *Murder trials*, p. 253.

110 *NW*, 18 March 1833.

111 Muir and Ruggiero, 'Introduction', p. vii.

112 Ball, *The judges in Ireland*, p. 342.

3. 'SO MISCHIEVOUS AND UNMANAGEABLE A CHARACTER'

1 *NW*, 18 March 1833.

2 W.E. Vaughan, *Murder trials in Ireland, 1836–1914* (Dublin, 2009), p. 118.

3 Ibid., p. 281; Peter Gray and Olwen Purdue, 'Introduction: the Irish lord lieutenancy, c.1541–1922' in Peter Gray and Olwen Purdue (eds), *The Irish lord lieutenancy, c.1541–1922* (Cork, 2012), pp 1–14 at 2.

4 *NW*, 18 March 1833.

5 *BNL* and *GCA*, 19 March 1833; Peter Gray and Olwen Purdue, 'Appendix: the chief governors of Ireland, 1541–1922' in Gray and Purdue (eds), *The Irish lord lieutenancy*, pp 233–7 at 236; 'Proceedings book "A" of Belfast District Lunatic Asylum, 1829–1844' (PRONI, HOS/28/1/2/1), pp 102 and 105 (henceforth cited as 'Proceedings book').

6 Catherine L. Evans, 'At her majesty's pleasure: criminal insanity in 19th-century Britain', *History Compass*, 14 (2016), 470–9 at 474.

7 Ibid., 474–5; Joseph Melling and Bill Forsyth, *The politics of madness: the state, insanity and society in England, 1845–1914* (London, 2005), pp 3–6.

8 Catherine Cox, *Negotiating insanity in the southeast of Ireland, 1820–1900* (Manchester, 2012), p. xvi. See also Jade Shepherd, 'Life for the families of the Victorian criminally insane', *Historical Journal* ('First View'), 1–30 at 2, available online at https://www.cambridge.org/core/journals/historical-journal/article/life-for-the-families-of-the-victorian-criminally-insane/05EBDCC620BA749C4323F178435A4F4F (accessed 17 April 2020); Oonagh Walsh, 'Lunatics and criminal alliances in nineteenth-century Ireland' in Peter Bartlett and

David Wright (eds), *Outside the walls of the asylum: the history of care in the community, 1750–2000* (London, 1999), pp 132–52 at 132–3.

9 Mark Finnane, *Insanity and the insane in post-Famine Ireland* (London, 1981), p. 14.

10 This account draws on Finnane, *Insanity and the insane*, pp 19–31; R.J. McClelland, 'The madhouses and mad doctors of Ulster', *Ulster Medical Journal*, 57 (1988), 101–20 at 102–7, 110–12; Malcolm, *History*, p. 90; Cox, *Negotiating insanity*, pp 1–6.

11 P.D. Hardy (ed.), *Twenty-one views in Belfast and its neighbourhood* (Dublin, 1837; repr. Belfast, 2005), p. 34; Gillespie and Royle, *Belfast*, p. 32; McClelland, 'Madhouses and mad doctors', 110.

12 Malcolm, *History*, pp 58, 90. See also McClelland, 'Madhouses and mad doctors', 110; R.W.M. Strain, *Belfast and its Charitable Society: a story of urban social development* (London, 1961), p. 289.

13 Finnane, *Insanity and the insane*, p. 19; Cox, *Negotiating insanity*, p. xii; Alvin Jackson, 'Ireland, the union and the empire, 1800–1960' in Kevin Kenny (ed.), *Ireland and the British Empire* (Oxford, 2004), pp 123–53 at 124–5; David Fitzpatrick, 'Ireland and the Empire' in Andrew Porter (ed.), *The Oxford history of the British Empire, volume III: the nineteenth century* (Oxford, 1999), pp 494–521 at 495–6.

14 Finnane, *Insanity and the insane*, p. 19.

15 Pauline Prior and David Griffiths, 'The chaplaincy question: the lord lieutenant of Ireland versus the Belfast Lunatic Asylum', *Eire-Ireland*, 32 (Summer/Fall, 1997), 137–53 at 137, 150–1, 152.

16 Ibid., 139, 152.

17 'Certificate of James Erskine Governor of Carrickfergus Gaol' (NAI, CRF 1838, Misc 10) (MFS/59/11).

18 'Proceedings book', p. 105; Malcolm, *History*, p. 91; D.R. Fisher (ed.), *The history of parliament, the House of Commons 1820–1932* (7 vols, Cambridge, 2009), v, p. 325.

19 'Proceedings book', p. 149.

20 Ibid., p. 107.

21 Ibid., p. 109.

22 'Certificate of James Erskine Governor of Carrickfergus Gaol' (NAI, CRF 1838,

Misc 10) (MFS/59/11); 'Proceedings book', p. 142.

23 *Twelfth report of the inspectors general on the general state of the prisons in Ireland: 1834*, HC 1834 (63), xl, 38.

24 'Proceedings book', p. 142.

25 Ibid., p. 145.

26 *Eleventh report of the inspectors general on the general state of the prisons in Ireland: 1833*, HC 1833 (67), xvii, 35; *Twelfth report … prisons in Ireland: 1834*, 38.

27 'Proceedings book', p. 146; T.W. Moody, F.X. Martin and F.J. Byrne (eds), *A new history of Ireland; ix, maps, genealogies, lists: a companion to Irish history part ii* (Oxford, 1984), p. 531.

28 'Proceedings book', p. 146.

29 Ibid., p. 149.

30 Ibid.

31 Gray and Purdue, 'Appendix: the chief governors of Ireland', p. 236.

32 Peter Gray, 'A "people's viceroyalty"? Popularity, theatre and executive politics, 1835–47' in Gray and Purdue (eds), *The Irish lord lieutenancy*, pp 158–78 at 159, 164–5. See also, for Mulgrave's popularity, M.A.G. Ó Tuathaigh, *Thomas Drummond and the government of Ireland, 1835–41* (Dublin, 1979), pp 4–5; Virginia Crossman, 'Phipps, Constantine Henry' in *DIB*.

33 *BNL*, 27 Oct. 1835; Gray, 'A "people's viceroyalty"?', p. 164.

34 *BNL*, 27 Oct. 1835.

35 'Proceedings book', p. 178.

36 Ibid., p. 182; *NW*, 26 Nov. 1835.

37 Cox, *Negotiating insanity*, p. xvi.

38 Ibid., pp xvi, 240–1.

39 Virginia Crossman, 'The growth of the state in the nineteenth century' in James Kelly (ed.), *The Cambridge history of Ireland, vol. III: 1730–1880* (Cambridge, 2018), pp 542–66 at 542–3, 566.

40 David N. Livingstone, *Putting science in its place: geographies of scientific knowledge* (Chicago, 2003), pp 68–72.

41 Ibid., p. 71.

42 Hardy (ed.), *Twenty-one views*, p. 34.

43 McClelland, 'Madhouses and mad doctors', 109; Livingstone, *Putting science in its place*, p. 68.

44 McClelland, 'Madhouses and mad doctors', 107.

45 'Proceedings book', pp 160, 164.

46 McClelland, 'Madhouses and mad doctors', 113.

47 Roger Cooter, *The cultural meaning of popular science: phrenology and the organization of consent in nineteenth-century Britain* (Cambridge, 1984), pp 279, 394; Reggie Chamberlain-King, *Weird Belfast: a miscellany, almanack and companion* (Belfast, 2014), p. 86.

48 Cooter, *Cultural meaning*, p. 3.

49 Ibid., pp 2, 124, 360n12.

50 Jonathan Jeffrey Wright and Diarmid A. Finnegan, 'Rocks, skulls and materialism: geology and phrenology in late-Georgian Belfast', *Notes and Records: the Royal Society Journal of the History of Science*, 72 (2018), 25–55 at 37–40. For phrenology in Ireland more broadly, see Enda Leaney, 'Phrenology in nineteenth-century Ireland', *New Hibernia Review*, 10 (Autumn, 2006), 24–42.

51 Wright and Finnegan, 'Rocks, skulls and materialism', 39–46.

52 *Testimonials on behalf of George Combe, as a candidate for the chair of logic in the University of Edinburgh* (Edinburgh, 1836), p. 8; Malcolm, *History*, pp 125–7 (126 for quote). For Combe, see Cooter, *Cultural meaning*, pp 101–33.

53 Malcolm, *History*, p. 91.

54 R.C., 'Case', 207.

55 Ibid., 209.

56 Ibid., 211, 212.

57 M.H. Kaufman and Robert McNeil, 'Death masks and life masks at Edinburgh University', *British Medical Journal*, 298 (1989), 506–7 at 506.

58 R.C., 'Case', 210.

59 Ibid., 209, 210; *NW*, 18 March 1833.

60 R.C., 'Case', 210.

61 Ibid.

62 'Proceedings book', p. 173.

63 Ibid., pp 153, 178, 182.

64 'The Petition of John Linn now confined in the Belfast District Lunatic Asylum' (NAI, CRF 1837, Misc 5) (MFS/59/08).

65 'Proceedings book', p. 182.

66 *GCA*, 24 Nov. 1835; *NW*, 26 Nov. 1835; *BNL*, 27 Nov. 1835.

67 *NW*, 26 Nov. 1835.

68 *FJ*, 3 Sept. 1836.

69 *NW*, 5 Sept. 1836.

70 *The Standard*, 5 Sept. 1836. See also the *Blackburn Standard*, 14 Sept. 1836.

71 *Caledonian Mercury*, 8 Sept. 1836.

72 'The Petition of John Lynn … at present confined in Carrickfergus Gaol' (NAI, CRF 1837, Misc 5) (MFS/59/08).

73 'The Petition of John Linn now confined in the Belfast District Lunatic Asylum' (NAI, CRF 1837, Misc 5) (MFS/59/08).

74 Strain, *Belfast and its Charitable Society*, pp 18–19; Hardy (ed.), *Twenty-one views*, p. 32.

75 Strain, *Belfast and its Charitable Society*, p. 112.

76 'Committee Book' of the Belfast Charitable Society, entry for 7 June 1834 (PRONI, MIC61/6). This source gives only the name of the girls' mother, Susannah Linn, but Martha Linn is identified elsewhere as John Linn's daughter.

77 Strain, *Belfast and its Charitable Society*, pp 124–5; 'Committee Book' of the Belfast Charitable Society, entry for 9 May 1835 (PRONI, MIC61/6); Mary McNeill, *The life and Times of Mary Ann McCracken, 1770–1866* (Belfast, 1988), p. 277.

78 Shepherd, 'Life for the families', 13.

79 'Registry Book' of Clifton Street Cemetery, pp 12 and 20, available online at http://www.belfasthistoryproject.com/cliftonstreetcemetery/ (accessed 1 Sept. 2019).

80 Shepherd, 'Life for the families', 18.

81 'Proceedings book', p. 212.

82 Ibid., p. 214.

83 *NW*, 12 Sept. 1836.

84 'Kilmainham Prison General Register 1835–1837 (Book No: 1/10/3)', entry 709 (NAI, accessible via Find My Past); 'Certificate of James Erskine Governor of Carrickfergus Gaol' (NAI, CRF 1838, Misc 10) (MFS/59/11).

85 'Certificate of James Erskine Governor of Carrickfergus Gaol' (NAI, CRF 1838, Misc 10) (MFS/59/11).

86 Keith Haines, 'Carrickfergus gaol conspiracy 1838', *Due North*, 1 (Oct. 1999), 3–9 at 6–7; *Fourth report of the inspectors general on the general state of the prisons of Ireland: 1826*, HC 1826 (173), xxiii, 23. For the reports of the inspectors general and prison reform, see Crossman, 'The growth of the state', pp 549–50.

87 *Fifth report of the inspectors general on the general state of the prisons of Ireland: 1827*,

HC 1826–27 (471), xi, 25; *Seventh report of the inspectors general on the general state of the prisons of Ireland: 1829*, HC 1829 (10), xiii, 31.

88 Haines, 'Carrickfergus gaol conspiracy', 8; *Report on the state of the prisons in Ireland*, HL 1820 (104), cxv, 9.

89 *Report of inspectors general; 1823: with abstract from appendix of general observations on each prison, in the several districts, &c.*, HC 1823 (342), x, 25.

90 *Report of the inspectors general on the general state of the prisons of Ireland: 1824*, HC 1824 (294), xxii, 27; *Report of the inspectors general on the general state of the prisons of Ireland: 1825*, HC 1825 (493), xxii, 24.

91 *Fourth report … prisons of Ireland: 1826*, 23.

92 *Eighth report of the inspectors general on the general state of the prisons of Ireland: 1830*, HC 1830 (48), xxiv, 30.

93 Haines, 'Carrickfergus gaol conspiracy', 8.

94 *Fifteenth report of the inspectors general on the general state of the prisons of Ireland, 1836: with appendixes*, HC 1837 (123), xxxi, 19.

95 *Eleventh report … prisons in Ireland: 1833*, 35.

96 *BNL*, 16 March 1838.

97 'Report of Local Inspector of County Antrim Gaol' (NAI, CRF 1838, Misc 10) (MFS/59/11).

98 Haines, 'Carrickfergus gaol conspiracy', 6.

99 *BNL*, 24 Sept. 1816.

100 *BNL*, 31 Dec. 1816.

101 *Report on the state of the prisons …* HL, 9.

102 Ibid., 18, 24, 60, 138, 166.

103 *Fourth report … prisons of Ireland: 1826*, 32, 47.

104 *Eighth report … prisons of Ireland: 1830*, 33–4, 45, 55, 64, 67; *Fifteenth report … prisons of Ireland, 1836: with appendixes*, 45.

105 'Information taken by and before Wm Burleigh and Edward Bruce' (NAI, CRF 1838, Misc 10) (MFS/59/11), statement of James Erskine.

106 Ibid.

107 Ibid., statement of John Crossan.

108 Ibid., statements of Michael Walter Cash, Bernard McAnnally and Patrick McMillan.

109 Ibid., statement of John Crossan.

110 Ibid., statement of Patrick McMillan.

111 Ibid., statement of John Crossan.

112 Ibid., statement of Michael Walter Cash.

113 Ibid., statements of John Crossan, Michael Walter Cash and Bernard McAnnaly.

114 *NW*, 8 Feb. 1838.

115 'Information taken by and before Wm Burleigh and Edward Bruce' (NAI, CRF 1838, Misc 10) (MFS/59/11), statement of Robert Forbes.

116 Ibid., statement of Michael Walter Cash.

117 *BNL*, 16 March 1838.

118 'Statement of Magistrates and Members of the Board of Superintendence respecting conspiracy in the Gaol of Carrickfergus' (NAI, CRF 1838, Misc 10) (MFS/59/11).

119 'Report' and 'Under Secretary's directions to Crown Solicitor' (NAI, CRF 1838, Misc 10) (MFS/59/11); Virginia Crossman, 'Drummond, Thomas' in *DIB*. See also, Ó Tuathaigh, *Thomas Drummond*.

120 'Under Secretary's directions to Crown Solicitor' (NAI, CRF 1838, Misc 10) (MFS/59/11).

121 Ibid.

122 'Copy of Opinion' (NAI, CRF 1838, Misc 10) (MFS/59/11).

123 'Report' (NAI, CRF 1838, Misc 10) (MFS/59/11).

124 *Eighth annual report*, p. 7.

125 *BNL*, 16 March 1838.

126 'Kilmainham Prison General Register 1836–1840 (Book No: 1/10/3)', entry 1399 (NAI, accessible via Find My Past).

127 'Diary of occurrences on board the convict ship Clyde', p. 8 (NLA, MS 6169), available online at https://catalogue.nla.gov.au/Record/2084065 (accessed 8 April 2020). Page number refers to online PDF.

128 Ibid., pp 12, 50, 51; 'John Lynn [Linn] Record ID cin47776', available online at https://www.digitalpanopticon.org/life?id=cin47776 (accessed 7 Nov. 2019).

CONCLUSION

1   Keith Haines, 'Carrickfergus gaol conspiracy 1838', *Due North*, 1 (Oct. 1999), 3–9 at 9.

2 Angélique Day and Patrick McWilliams, *Ordnance survey memoirs of Ireland, vol. 37: parishes of County Antrim xiv, 1832, 1839–40: Carrickfergus* (Belfast, 1996), p. 150.

3 *NW*, 30 July 1839. See also, *BNL*, 2 Aug. 1839.

4 *BNL*, 9 Aug. 1839.

5 *NW*, 29 Oct. 1839 (the name is given here as Crossen, but it is clear that Crossan is referred to).

6 'Information taken by and before Wm Burleigh and Edward Bruce' (NAI, CRF 1838, Misc 10) (MFS/59/11), statement of James Erskine; *BNL*, 16 March 1838.

7 Malcolm, *History*, pp 91–2; Pauline Prior, 'Gender and criminal lunacy in nineteenth century Ireland' in Margaret H. Preston and Margaret Ó hÓgartaigh (eds), *Gender and medicine in Ireland, 1700–1950* (Syracuse, NY, 2012), pp 86–107 at 87. See also, for the Dundrum asylum, Pauline M. Prior, 'Murder and madness: gender and the insanity defence in nineteenth-century Ireland', *New Hibernia Review*, 9 (Winter, 2005), 19–36 (esp. 20–1); Pauline M. Prior, 'Prisoner or patient? The official debate on the criminal lunatic in nineteenth-century Ireland', *History of Psychiatry*, 15 (2004), 177–92.

8 Malcolm, *History*, p. 92.

9 Prior, 'Gender and criminal lunacy', p. 87.

10 *Eighth annual report*, pp 6–7.

11 *NW*, 12 June 1838; Catherine Cox, *Negotiating insanity in the southeast of Ireland, 1820–1900* (Manchester, 2012), pp 76.

12 *NW*, 28 May 1839.

13 *BNL*, 16 May 1862.

14 *BNL*, 25 and 28 July 1862.

15 *Ulster Magazine and Monthly Review of Science and Literature*, 3 (1862), 341–5 at 342.

16 *NW*, 17 Dec. 1850.

17 Thomas Gaffikin, *Belfast fifty years ago. A lecture, delivered by Thomas Gaffikin, in the Working Men's Institute, Belfast on Thursday Evg., April 8th, 1875, James Alex. Henderson, Esq., J.P. (ex-mayor of Belfast), in the chair* (Belfast, 1894), p. 3.

18 Ibid., p. 41.

19 Ibid., pp 16, 29, 31.

20 Ibid., pp 14, 15, 38, 41.

21 Ibid., p. 3.

22 For Cobb and his work, see Cesare Cuttica, 'Anti-methodology par excellence: Richard Cobb (1917–96) and history writing', *European Review of History*, 21 (2014), 91–110 and Colin Jones, 'Richard Charles Cobb (1917–1996)', *Biographical Memoirs of the British Academy*, 14 (2015), 88–117, available online at https://www.thebritishacademy.ac.uk/publications/memoirs/cobb-richard-charles-1917-1996 (accessed 13 April 2020).

23 Richard Cobb, *A sense of place* (London, 1975), pp 3–4 and (for 'L'Affaire Perken') 51–76.